Becoming-Teacher

IMAGINATION AND PRAXIS: CRITICALITY AND CREATIVITY IN EDUCATION AND EDUCATIONAL RESEARCH

VOLUME 12

SCOPE

Current educational reform rhetoric around the globe repeatedly invokes the language of 21st century learning and innovative thinking while contrarily re-enforcing, through government policy, high stakes testing and international competition, standardization of education that is exceedingly reminiscent of 19th century Taylorism and scientific management. Yet, as the steam engines of educational "progress" continue down an increasingly narrow, linear, and unified track, it is becoming increasingly apparent that the students in our classrooms are inheriting real world problems of economic instability, ecological damage, social inequality, and human suffering. If young people are to address these social problems, they will need to activate complex, interconnected, empathetic and multiple ways of thinking about the ways in which peoples of the world are interconnected as a global community in the living ecosystem of the world. Seeing the world as simultaneously local, global, political, economic, ecological, cultural and interconnected is far removed from the Enlightenment's objectivist and mechanistic legacy that presently saturates the status quo of contemporary schooling. If we are to derail this positivist educational train and teach our students to see and be in the world differently, the educational community needs a serious dose of imagination. The goal of this book series is to assist students, practitioners, leaders, and researchers in looking beyond what they take for granted, questioning the normal, and amplifying our multiplicities of knowing, seeing, being and feeling to, ultimately, envision and create possibilities for positive social and educational change. The books featured in this series will explore ways of seeing, knowing, being, and learning that are frequently excluded in this global climate of standardized practices in the field of education. In particular, they will illuminate the ways in which imagination permeates every aspect of life and helps develop personal and political awareness. Featured works will be written in forms that range from academic to artistic, including original research in traditional scholarly format that addresses unconventional topics (e.g., play, gaming, ecopedagogy, aesthetics), as well as works that approach traditional and unconventional topics in unconventional formats (e.g., graphic novels, fiction, narrative forms, and multi-genre texts). Inspired by the work of Maxine Greene, this series will showcase works that "break through the limits of the conventional" and provoke readers to continue arousing themselves and their students to "begin again" (Greene, *Releasing the Imagination*, 1995, p. 109).

Becoming-Teacher

A Rhizomatic Look at First-Year Teaching

Kathryn J. Strom
California State University, East Bay, USA

and

Adrian D. Martin
New Jersey City University, USA

SENSE PUBLISHERS
ROTTERDAM/BOSTON/TAIPEI

A C.I.P. record for this book is available from the Library of Congress.

ISBN: 978-94-6300-870-9 (paperback)
ISBN: 978-94-6300-871-6 (hardback)
ISBN: 978-94-6300-872-3 (e-book)

Published by: Sense Publishers,
P.O. Box 21858,
3001 AW Rotterdam,
The Netherlands
https://www.sensepublishers.com/

All chapters in this book have undergone peer review.

Printed on acid-free paper

This book is dedicated to Ana Maria Villegas. Without your mentorship, critique, encouragement, and love, this work would not have been possible.

TABLE OF CONTENTS

ACKNOWLEDGEMENTS

We would like to acknowledge Monica Taylor and Emily Klein for their mentorship. We learned so much about teacher education pedagogy from you.

We'd also like to thank Linda Abrams, Charity Dacey, and Tammy Mills for their unwavering support & love.

CHALLENGING SIMPLISTIC NARRATIVES WITH RHIZOMATICS

On December 8, 2008, the cover of the US magazine *Newsweek* featured the headline, "How to Fix America's Schools." Next to the white lettering of this grandiose statement, and against the backdrop of a school classroom, stood a black power-suited Michelle Rhee, brandishing a broom. At the time, Rhee was the chancellor of the District of Columbia Public Schools in Washington, D.C. and was (in)famous for firing teachers in large numbers as a district turn-around strategy. The message from *Newsweek,* which began to echo around the nation, was clear: *teachers* were to blame for America's educational woes, and the way to solve the problem was to clean house. Simple enough.

In 2008, we, Adrian and Katie, were still K-12 classroom teachers. Adrian taught elementary school in Passaic, New Jersey, and Katie taught seventh and eighth grade history in San Diego, California. Both of us worked primarily with students of color and English learners in high-poverty neighborhoods. Although we taught on opposite sides of the country, we faced the same simplistic narrative: our schools had been labeled as "failing" under the 2001 No Child Left Behind, and our responsibility was to make sure that our students raised their test scores. End of story.

Except it was not the end of the story—it was only the beginning. From our own experiences, we understood that no one-to-one correspondences existed between our actions as teachers and our students' test scores. There were so many aspects of the process that did not figure into this simple perspective of "failure." Take our students, for example. Even before they entered our classrooms for the day, many of them were dealing with circumstances beyond their control that impacted their ability to come to school consistently, much less participate in class productively. Thirteen-year-old Janae, for example, missed school several times a month to take care of her little sister, because her mother had to work and could not afford childcare for her infant daughter. Ismael, who had to walk his younger sister to school through multiple gang territories, brought a knife for protection one day and missed an entire week of school out on suspension. The father of another student, Jacky, had been recently incarcerated and her schoolwork fell to the side as she tried to find a way to cope. These circumstances, unsurprisingly, affected the ways they responded to us and our teaching.

Beyond these side effects of poverty, students of color and English learner (EL) students attend a punitive school system that tells them every day that they are problems to be fixed. When they speak non-dominant varieties of English or their heritage languages, we tell them that they need to speak *proper English*. We place them in remedial, special education, and low-track classes at much higher rates than their white peers. We force them to enter their schools though metal detectors and house police officers on campuses in low-income neighborhoods, sending the message that we consider them to be criminals. We present them with a curriculum that tells them that their histories, cultures, and ways of understanding the world do not matter (or in some cases, that they do not even exist). Then, we tell them that if they only work hard in school, that hard work will translate into prosperity—although the evidence of that myth is apparent from the people in their communities who did go to school and work hard, and still have been excluded from opportunities to succeed economically. With these daily experiences, it is no wonder that many students of color and ELs have no desire to participate in a system that continually reinforces their oppression, and might not respond to instruction in ways that teachers desire.

The simplistic narrative adopted by proponents of the neoliberal reform agenda, like Michelle Rhee, does not consider other factors besides the teacher that influence the relationship between teaching and student achievement, such as the students themselves, their histories and daily realities, and the ways they interact with the punitive structures of schooling. By filtering out all elements except the teacher and assigning a causal relation between the teacher and learning, this perspective of teaching positions the teacher as an autonomous actor, students as passive, and contexts as neutral. Across the world the paradigm of neoliberalism has taken hold of K-12 and teacher education, not only producing schooling conditions that constrain early career (and indeed, all) teachers in enacting socially just teaching, but also perpetuating linear patterns of thought, which are underlined by the logic of the market.

Over the next few years, as we left the classroom and entered our doctoral studies, we began to realize that a major part of the problem was the simplistic thinking that informed this wave of neoliberal reforms being implemented in schools. We wondered what it might look like to study teaching from a complex perspective, one that took into consideration the multiple moving parts that influence the work of the teacher, including herself, her students, and the conditions present in her school setting. These wonderings eventually brought us to Deleuze and Guattari's work with rhizomatics, and we have been "thinking with" Deleuzoguattarian concepts ever since. Thus, this book is as much about the process of becoming-teacher itself as it is about thinking about such processes, and indeed, thinking in general.

In this book, we put several rhizomatic concepts to work to generate different accounts of teaching, accounts that begin with assumptions of multiplicity instead of individual autonomy, and quasi-causality rather than one-to-one correspondence, to interrupt linear thinking patterns about teaching/learning to teach. Rhizomatics offers a language with which to "make the familiar strange," but the sheer volume of new terms introduced in Deleuze's work and Deleuze and Guattari's collaborations requires a fair amount of study, and thus renders these concepts inaccessible to many.

This in itself is ironic, as Deleuze himself encouraged others to resist a search for deeper meaning when reading his works, since there was none to be found. Instead, he encouraged his readers to ask themselves what the concepts he presented could do for them—how the ideas might be put to work. Despite the sometimes slippery nature of Deleuzoguattarian philosophy, we are convinced that rhizomatics does lend itself to practical use, and in the following pages, we will attempt to persuade our readers of the pragmatics of this project. As we do so, we invite you to think of yourself as forming an assemblage with this book—that is, to come into composition and "plug" yourself into it, to create a machine (Deleuze & Guattari, 1987). Take out of it ideas that you can think with productively, and overall, *differently,* in your own context(s).

We have organized the book into eight chapters. We begin by providing an overview of the main rhizomatic concepts we use in this book (we revisit these in each of the chapters and explain them throughout to provide multiple entry points into the ideas). We then turn to the pedagogical and empirical grounding for the study, discussing teaching for social justice and the challenges new teachers tend to experience as they attempt to enact equitable practices in their first year in the classroom. In the third chapter, we discuss our process of rhizomatic inquiry, describing the methodological perspectives and approaches that guided our study. The following chapters present the cases of our three teacher participants, Mauro, Bruce, and June, discussing their construction of practices read through a rhizomatic lens. The final two chapters present a cross-case discussion and offer implications for using insights drawn from these cases to inform teacher education practice, supports in schools, policy, and research regarding new teachers.

THINKING RHIZOMATICALLY IN AN
ERA OF NEOLIBERALISM

INTRODUCTION

During his instructional unit on evolution, Mauro, a first year science teacher, had an exciting idea for introducing his lesson on natural selection to his ninth grade environmental science class. He went to Costco and bought a tub filled with approximately 80 pieces of a wide variety of well known candies: miniature bags of M&Ms and Skittles, Tootsie Rolls, Laffy Taffy, Smarties, Twizzlers, snack-size Snickers and Almond Joy bars, and flavored lollipops. His idea was to have each student choose two pieces of candy, which would leave about twenty leftover pieces. Mauro would use these leftover pieces as an entry point to the idea of natural selection, pointing out that the types of candy leftover were less attractive to predators (the students). If the leftover candy reproduced, the offspring would more likely possess characteristics of the leftover candy than the candy consumed by the predators. As class began, Mauro gave students directions and passed around the tub. When it made its way back to him, the tub contained only two pieces of candy—students had taken more than their two allotted pieces, and Mauro's carefully planned lesson introduction was ruined.

Anyone who has spent time working in P-12 classrooms would concede to the often unpredictable nature of teaching activity. As we see in the vignette above, teachers create instructional units and learning experiences for students, but they are not the only variables with agency acting in a learning situation. In order to enact the kinds of learning experiences they created and devised, teachers rely on students to follow their instructions, participate in activities in particular ways, communicate with one another at specific times, and negotiate a variety of other observable activity in the classroom. However, teachers are also simultaneously navigating a host of other, often invisible elements—their own understandings of good teaching, expectations embedded within their school culture, societal norms of student behavior, a finite block of time allotted for a lesson—just to name a few. As the above vignette illustrates, teaching is co-constructed—it is not simply an action "done" by a teacher. Rather, teaching is an active and evolving series of activities that unfold within the classroom, co-constructed and negotiated among participants (e.g., students and teachers), influenced by and influencing a variety of elements both observable and non-observable, within both local and widespread contexts.

While this idea might seem to be "common sense" for those of us who have spent years working with P-12 students, dominant ways of conceptualizing teaching in the current era of neoliberalism provide a different message. Consistent with tenets of neoliberalism, which emphasize entrepreneurialism, individualism, and self-regulation (Harvey, 2005), recent education policies and reforms position the teacher as an autonomous actor uninfluenced by the formerly discussed elements who "does" teaching to students. In other words, academic content is provided in a cause-effect transaction in which teachers "dispense" knowledge and information to students, who are passive recipients of that information. This view assumes that the learning experienced during preservice education by teacher candidates is an object that is transferred, whole and unchanged, into the in-service classroom without interference or modifications. When teachers fail to implement the type of practices they learned about in their teacher preparation programs (as research on first year teachers show they often do), proponents of neoliberally influenced, market-driven reforms claim teacher education to be ineffective and superfluous. This critique espoused by supporters of market-driven reforms and policies—which some maintain is a direct attempt to dismantle university-based teacher education (Sleeter, 2008; Zeichner, 2010b)—has led to the call for alternate teacher credentialing and the proliferation of programs like "Teach for America" that put individuals with little or no teaching preparation into classrooms.

In the chapters that follow, we aim to disrupt this either-or, zero-sum type of rhetoric about the enactment of teacher learning and practice—that is, that teachers either "do" the learning they "acquired" during preservice education (and thus teacher education is worthwhile); or it is completely "washed out" (Zeichner & Tabachnik, 1981) (failing to manifest in the in-service context, rendering preparatory experiences and preservice learning completely worthless). We present this argument through the cases of three first-year teachers, exploring the ways that they constructed their practices over the first several months of their new careers (we define "practices" as the cognitive and physical acts that comprise the process of teaching). As we develop the cases, we draw on concepts from rhizomatics (Deleuze & Guattari, 1987)—a non-linear philosophy that seeks to interrupt linear, normative ways of thinking about human phenomena, ontology, and epistemology. Rhizomatic concepts serve as analytic tools that provide a more complex, nuanced interpretation of the multiplicity and composition of elements that constitute the nature of teaching.

TEACHING AND TEACHER EDUCATION IN AN ERA OF NEOLIBERALISM

In relation to education, the neoliberal era has ushered in the "Corporate Education Reform Movement," a series of governmentally-imposed policies and systems driven by the logic of the free market (Karp, 2010; Ravitch, 2011/2013) that is, notably, supported across the political party spectrum. Front and center in this movement is the notion that accountability and competition will increase educational quality and equity. In other words, schools should be held accountable for student performance, as measured via standardized assessment, to ensure quality control. Moreover, proponents of the corporate education movement promote the idea that attaching financial rewards and sanctions based on that standardized test performance will increase competition among schools, resulting in overall improvement in our education systems at all levels. Hence, all public schools must now engage in standardized testing at increasing levels to maintain funding and avoid financial sanctions. Drawing from this same logic, policy makers and reformers have connected (or are seeking to connect) teacher evaluations to student achievement based on standardized assessments. Ultimately, the use of standardized testing results to significantly inform teacher evaluation and as a deciding factor in school funding has led to narrow, prescribed curriculum focused on standardized testing preparation, diminishing the ability to enact learner-centered, student-driven instruction and messaging its implementation as onerous or impossible (Sleeter, 2009).

In conjunction with these policies and reforms, the neoliberal free-market principle that privatization increases competition has driven the school "choice" movement in education. Throughout the nation, the choice movement has led to the proliferation of charter schools, which has, in many cities, drained funding from local school municipalities to the detriment of community public schools. Charter schools, almost all of which are non-unionized, also support the political movement to suppress worker organizing through the dismantling of unions (teachers represent the largest unionized force in the US). Ultimately, the charter movement is centered on privatizing education, maintaining it as a commodity to be bought and sold in accord with the whim of the market instead of a public good to which all members of society are entitled (Ravitch, 2013).

This corporate education movement has not just affected P-12 education, however. The neoliberal agendas that inform this movement have enabled a systematic attack on teacher education programs that require teacher candidates to study pedagogy and complete extended practica (Zeichner, 2010b). Claiming that licensing and preparation requirements for teachers dissuade talented parties from entering the field of education, and coupled with "research" suggesting that teacher education bears no influence in the actual practice of teaching, critics of university-based teacher preparation have called for alternate entryways (also known as "fast-track" programs) into the occupation of teaching. The past two decades have seen a proliferation of these programs that effectively deprofessionalizes teaching. Normally requiring only a bachelor's degree, these alternate route programs profess to specialize in "on-the-job" training, with minimal study of pedagogy, teaching and learning, or guided practice in the application of instructional skills prior to becoming a teacher of record (Klein, Taylor, Onore, Strom, & Abrams, 2013).

With an increasingly narrow curricular focus on the knowledge and skills assessed in standardized measures for which schools are increasingly held financially accountable, the combination of the aforementioned neoliberal reforms, policies and programs also have pressured teacher education and P-12 systems to remove social justice, culturally responsive and relevant instruction, and/or multicultural emphases

(Sleeter, 2009). However, despite neoliberal proponent claims that they aim to increase equitable learning experiences for students, research that has emerged over the last several years suggests that the educational reforms stemming from the corporate education movement present major social justice issues. In particular, children of color, ELs, and special needs students, as well as those living in poverty, are disproportionately harmed by these policies.

Schools that serve large populations of underserved students tend to be located in predominantly socioeconomically low income areas, and thus are more likely to be underfunded and under-resourced, given that public schools are primarily funded by the local district. With the high concentration of diverse student populations, the underfunding of schools, and a variety of other factors, schools in these areas are also more likely to "fail" on standardized measures of student learning in comparison to peer institutions that serve predominantly mainstream, middle and upper-class populations. At present, even ELs and special needs students are required to take standardized tests despite research that raises serious concerns about the appropriateness of this practice and whether these tests actually measure what they purport to (Darling-Hammond, 2007; Au, 2008). Because student achievement on these standardized measures is overwhelmingly low, these schools are disproportionately subject to financial sanctions, and forced to contend with curriculum reforms and a school culture that emphasize a narrow set of basic skills to be mastered in order to elevate standardized measures of learning. Moreover, while school "choice" is touted as a way to more effectively serve all students (including students of diverse backgrounds), studies have shown that nationwide, charter schools tend to underserve students living in poverty, students of color, ELs, and special needs students (CREDO, 2009). Because charter schools can exercise some autonomy and choice as to which students will attend these schools (often selecting students who demonstrate a capacity to score high on standardized measures), neighboring public schools are left serving the remaining student population with less funding and resources.

The confluence of these conditions further deprives students of meaningful, equitable, learner-centered educational experiences, given that qualified teachers are likely to be dissuaded from teaching in these settings, since their evaluations will be based on students' standardized testing performance as a prime consideration in their hiring, renewal, and attainment of tenure. Due to multiple factors, that performance is likely to be lower than in more affluent/white schools. Combined with the "revolving door" of teacher turnover in these schools (Ingersoll, 2003), the lack of interest in teaching in these schools creates the illusion of teacher shortage. Instead, alternate route teachers—those who have had little or no preparation or practice for teaching—are more likely to be employed in these "high needs" schools.

Even for those who do pursue professional preparation for teaching, the first year is notoriously difficult. New teachers often struggle to enact what they have learned in their preservice teacher education programs, while simultaneously learning to work with colleagues and the culture of their institutions. Support from mentors is often inconsistent, mismatched to content or grade level, or completely absent. Compounding these challenges, new teachers often receive the most challenging teaching assignments (e.g., Tait, 2008) and as previously noted, are more likely to work in high needs schools that are under-resourced and under-funded. As a result, new teachers often just struggle for survival, and tend to reproduce the transmission-based practices that contradict current understandings of equitable pedagogy. With these difficulties, new teachers play a large role in the "revolving door" mentioned above, with as many as half of new teachers leaving the profession by their fifth year of teaching.

As we explain below, rhizomatics (Deleuze & Guattari, 1987) provides a way to trouble linear thinking undergirding the neoliberal education movement—such as the causal relations that policymakers and others have assumed exist between students and tests, teaching and learning, and teaching and teacher preparation. By utilizing Deleuzian concepts to analyze the multiple interactions that take place in the first year of teaching, we can produce a more complex view of the role of teacher learning that occurs in initial teacher preparation, and thus develop an argument for its importance. We also argue that this philosophy provides productive tools with which to theorize a resistance to the neoliberal education movement at the classroom level, highlighting means of supporting teachers in enacting socially just practices and interrupting an educational paradigm detrimental to children most vulnerable to the neoliberal agenda.

THE TREE AND THE RHIZOME

The current neoliberal context enables and reinforces a particular type of thinking, which in turn influences a view of reality—and thus the way phenomena like teaching is socially, discursively, and psychologically conceptualized. This type of thinking, generally known as positivism, emerged from the Enlightenment and the scientific revolution, and is characterized by an objectivist epistemology and realist ontology (St. Pierre & Roulston, 2006). In short, this kind of thinking emphasizes that there is an objective reality that may be studied and ordered according to a universal set of rules; knowledge exists "out there" to be discovered; and humans are rational creatures whose existence (or ontology) is defined by their very rationality—"I think, therefore I am" (St. Pierre, 2000). Although positivistic views of knowledge and reality have been around for hundreds of years and are arguably the basis of Western thought patterns and scientific reasoning, their current resurgence in education as a mandatory orientation for quality research is noteworthy (St. Pierre, 2004).

The philosophy of rhizomatics seeks to disrupt this type of thought and posit an alternative (though not an opposite) view of thinking, of ontology, and of human experience. Deleuze and Guattari (1987) describe positivist thought as the "oldest and weariest kind of thought," a binary logic that "endlessly develops the law of the One that becomes two, then of the two that become four" (p. 5), always reducible to a universal essence, *the truth*. This type of thought is linear, sequential, ordered: it is the logic that underscores the notion that one person can observe a teacher teaching, analyze it along a checklist of criteria, and assign an either/or label: she is doing what she is supposed to, or she is not. She is effective or ineffective; Her lessons are teacher-led or student centered; her students are engaged or disengaged. Deleuze and Guattari label this mode of thought as arborescent or tree thought, asserting: "We are tired of trees...they've made us suffer too much. All of arborescent culture is founded on them" (36). Not only does this type of "petrified" thought dismiss other ways of knowing and being—which in our colonized world translates into the dismissal of indigenous and other subordinated populations' epistemologies and ontologies—but it is also a ruse, deceiving us into thinking/ believing that the current order of the world around us is the way that it has to be (Hinchey, 1998). Tree thought, because it only can reproduce itself—*the one that becomes two*—closes off other, perhaps previously unthought possibilities about existence, life experience, epistemology, and agency. It is the kind of thought that Barad (2007), quoting a poem by Alice Fulton, describes thus: "Because truths we don't suspect have a hard time making themselves felt" (p. 1).

To help begin to think differently and thus open a space for thinking previously unthought potentialities, Deleuze and Guattari offer the figuration of the *rhizome*— not as a metaphor, but rather as an analytic tool (as all their concepts are meant). A rhizome, as it appears in nature, is a bulbous plant or tuber that grows unpredictably in all directions, proceeding by offshoots. Other examples provided by these philosophers include strawberry plants, crabgrass, or a pack of rats. If tree logic operates via the binary in either/ors, rhizomes operate in *ands*, connecting and expanding rather than closing off or creating boundaries. In contrast to the tree, rhizomes are acentered multiplicities, composed of heterogenous elements that form connections and change as they come into composition, always in a fluid state of *becoming different* as they move from one threshold to another.

Thinking Differently with Rhizomatic Concepts

We assert that Deleuzian philosophy is useful for theorizing the complexity of teaching practice, and in particular, teaching for social justice. Not only does rhizomatics interrupt linear views of "transference" of teacher learning into practice, but it also disrupts dominant forms of instruction (discussed in the next chapter), which mimic the characteristics of arborescent structures. In transmission teaching, learning is unidirectional—the teacher fills the student with content knowledge and the student reflects this internalized knowledge on a test. In this model, the teacher is the tree trunk while the students are the branches, reproducing the information that teachers have given them.

However, rhizomatics offers multiple concepts with which to *think differently* about teaching, education, and life more generally. The language of rhizomatics breaks with fundamental notions of positivism, providing a vocabulary of multiples, fluidity, flux, expansion, and difference. Because of these characteristic foci, rhizomatics is concerned with *processes* over states—becoming over being—because, if the world indeed is always changing from one moment to the next, in a constant state of transformation (or becoming), studying *what is* would be a fruitless endeavor. By the time one has decided what *it is,* it would have become something else. Rather, rhizomatics focuses on questions that ask about context, function, and production. *How does it work? How does it work for you? What does it function with? What does it produce? What different thoughts does it produce or enable you to think?* (Deleuze & Guattari, 1987)

As outlined in the introduction, in this study we are strategic with the language that we draw from Deleuze. We focus on a cluster of concepts that we feel can help us address particular problems of thinking in teacher education—namely, the problem of linear thinking and the simplistic evaluation of the connection between teacher learning and teaching practice. These include the concepts of *assemblage, becoming,* and *rhizomatic lines* (molar, molecular, and lines of flight). In addition, we also use the term "multiplicity" to indicate a collective, and the adjective "multiplicitous" to connote the multiple nature of such collectives. We define each concept in the sections below.

Assemblage

The concept of assemblage both helps to express the multiplistic, co-constituted nature of teaching, as well as serve as a tool with which to analyze the interplay among various elements in the context of teaching and learning that jointly produce different kinds of teaching practice. An assemblage is an aggregate of elements, both human and non, that function collectively in a contextually unique manner to produce *something* (e.g., teaching practice, a situated identity). In this way, elements (humans, non-humans, actions, or events) are defined by their relations and functions as part of an assemblage, not by any inherent properties they possess.

To contextualize to teaching, a classroom is an assemblage, "composed of humans, writing implements, writing surfaces, texts, desks, doors, as well as disciplinary forces whose power and agency are elicited through various routines (e.g., singing the anthem) and references ('In algebra, we always do this …') (deFreitas, 2012, p. 562). In this assemblage, the students, teacher, physical space of the classroom, discourses, and behaviors function together to shape what the teacher and students collectively do/create. As such, the concept of assemblage lends itself to conceptualizing the work of the teacher not as a product enacted by an autonomous actor, but co-produced through a constellation of elements. Each element that composes the constellation is not held as separate, discrete, and neutral, but is conceived as an active agent in the joint production of the practices that are constructed. The collection of elements referenced at the onset of this paragraph thus functions and contributes toward a specific production and as such are integrally enmeshed, one with the other, in the activity that unfolds in the classroom.

Becoming

Within a rhizomatic frame, teaching practice—that is, the processes of teaching—is not a static property or engagement the teacher uses or does, but rather is co-constructed *becomings*, or transformations-in-action, produced by the collective workings of the teaching-assemblage. A becoming is "a verb with a consistency all its own" (Deleuze & Guattari, 1987, p. 239), expressing a happening rather than a thing. Rather than connoting an evolution toward an end point (or a defined developmental trajectory), this use of becoming is "involution" (p. 238), a creative function occurring between heterogeneous elements. Becomings are created through alliances, as bodies, ideas, forces, and other elements come into composition in assemblages, and produce something new, different. Therefore, becoming directly contradicts the notion of the teacher as an isolated, encapsulated body/mind acting completely on her own volition, presupposing the notion of 'being,' or the rational concept of a being existing in and of itself. Extending this concept to the classroom, *becoming-teacher* necessarily implicates not just the individual teacher, but all the elements, forces, bodies and ideas that make up the teaching-assemblage.

Becoming also helps to reframe identity in a way that expresses its dynamic nature. As other researchers in education have pointed out, teacher identity is an important consideration because of its impact on the work that occurs in the classroom (Achinstein & Ogawa, 2011; Britzman, 1991; Bullough, 2005; Lasky, 2005; Sloan, 2006). Contemporary research in education also recognizes the contextually constructed, multi-faceted, ever-shifting nature of teacher identity (Rogers & Scott, 2008; Zembylas, 2003). Rhizomatics shifts this poststructural notion of relational and fragmented self toward a relational and fragmented *becoming-self* process, an individuality that is an event rather than a being (Deleuze, 1990). In other words, this notion moves away from the "what" question of teacher identity, toward the "how and why" of identity construction—a look at identity-in-action, or the series of co-constructions that unfold, fold over, and refold in the becoming of a teacher.

In the classroom, conceptualizing a teacher identity construction *process* enables us to focus on what teachers do and are capable of doing in their assemblage, rather than what their identities are. Attending to teacher identity as becoming allows us to move away from the idea of a teacher as a stable, encapsulated body and instead toward an amalgam of "body-world-process" (Blackman, 2012). This perspective, then, opens the possibilities of understanding the relational, contextual, and collective processes that contribute to *becoming-teacher.* We suggest that *becoming-teacher* is a concept that provides an alternative to traditional notions of teacher learning and growth, an ongoing view of transformation that is non-linear, non-directional, and never quite actualized.

Rhizomatic Lines

Rhizomes are made up of "lines" that articulate how the elements comprising a multiplicity work or function. There are two main types of lines: molar and molecular. *Molar lines* are segmented and rigid, forces that "cut up" bodies, forcing them into acceptable patterns of behavior, institutional norms, and/or dominant ways of thinking and being in the world. Molar lines are dualisms, such as man/woman, black/white, rich/middle class/poor, and typologies or labels, like English Language Learner, At Risk student, or Disabled. Molar lines generally represent the macro-level of politics, although they are not just imposed from above. As Deleuze and Guattari caution, "It's easy to be anti-fascist on the molar level and not even see the fascist inside you" (p. 215). Molar lines thus encapsulate the presently accepted norms, rules, social structures, conventions, and forms of communication that, although socially constructed, are assumed as inherently "normal", "natural", functioning as the standard to which which all human activity and social phenomena are held. In education, examples of molar lines include bell schedules, grade levels, mandated curriculum, codes of conduct, ideas internalized by students' of what it means to be "good", and deep-set beliefs by teachers who profess to believe in student-centered learning but maintain a cultural script of the need to control their class ("the fascist inside you").

The second type of line is the supple, flexible *molecular line*, which carries out the work of the molar. This is the micropolitical line, the "supple fabric without which [the state's] rigid segments would not hold" (Deleuze & Guattari, 1987, p. 213). Just as a molar fascist dictatorship cannot be successful long-term without its citizens nourishing their internal fascists, institutional rules and societal status quos must also be carried out by people. Here Deleuze and Guattari bring in the notion of agency—although their treatment of agency does not refer to rational decision-making, or "a choice like you [might] think" (Dyke, 2013, p. 153). Molecular lines have the potential to support the status quo, observe the institutional norm, obey the school bell and follow the pacing guide. As you might imagine, much of the day-to-day work of the teacher must support institutional rules and structures. Thus, the individual thoughts, actions, and practices of teachers that feed into and reinforce the molar system are the molecular lines at work.

However, because of their suppleness, molecular lines also have the potential to escape the status quo and form a *line of flight*. Lines of flight are breaks from the molar—a subversion of the institutional norm or inner fascist. For Deleuze and Guattari, lines of flight spur regime change and define societies:

It is as if a line of flight, perhaps only a tiny trickle to begin with, leaked between segments, escaping their centralization, eluding their totalization. The profound movements stirring a society present themselves in this fashion... From the viewpoint of micropolitics, a society is defined by its lines of flight. (p. 216)

The fabric of everyday life in the classroom provides a multitude of opportunities for lines of flight. A student might pose an unexpected question that spurs the teacher to open a discussion for the class to explore, and they shoot off into previously unthought territory. A teacher might encourage her class to use non-gendered language, like "partner" in the place of "husband" or "wife." The class might discuss "testing" from a critical perspective. Each of these breaks or subverts the status quo in some way.

By nature, however, lines of flight are temporal. They will be recaptured by the molar line: "Molecular escapes would be nothing if they did not return to the molar organizations to reshuffle their segments, their binary distributions of sexes, classes, and parties" (p. 217). In the classroom, the teacher will eventually have to return to her original objective or give the test, and students will have to take it. The bell will ring and students will leave the class and go out into the world where they encounter heteronormative language at every turn. But in the recapture of lines of flight, the molar lines of the system are shuffled, and social change is possible. It is here, through the productive employment of lines of flight, that we theorize that teaching for social justice might take hold. Multiple lines of flight, reconstructed in classrooms over time, have the potential to disrupt neoliberal influences and enable a rethinking of teaching and learning that attends to the equitable inclusion of all individuals (teachers and students) and provide opportunities for the realization of both imagined and not-yet-thought becomings.

TEACHING AS RHIZOMATIC ACTIVITY

Our argument that teaching, and teaching for social justice in particular, is a complex activity is certainly not new. Education scholars have argued this point from the viewpoint of postmodernism (e.g., Hargreaves & Jacka, 1995), complexity theory (e.g., Clarke & Collins, 2007; Cochran-Smith et al., 2013), and social constructivism (e.g., Windschitl, 2002). Yet, we suggest that by using the rhizomatic concepts outlined above, we not only provide an explanatory framework for complex activities, but also analytic tools that push our understanding past "*what*" questions to the "*how*" of the construction of complex practice. The concepts of assemblage, becoming, and lines of flight are also theoretical tools that can be put to work from *inside* the neoliberal system—that is, they account for the dominant power structures (molar lines) and provide a space for them in theorizing teaching for social justice.

SOCIAL JUSTICE PEDAGOGY AND BEGINNING TEACHERS

Dominant, pervasive conceptualizations and the institutional culture and norms of schools are rigid, regulated, striated, and overcoded so individuals (teachers and students) participate in socially patterned behaviors and ways of thinking. From a rhizomatic perspective, schools are full of molar lines—including transmission teaching (the dispensing of information from the teacher to the student), which still serves as the dominant form of instruction, particularly in urban, high poverty settings (Haberman, 2010). Given that this form of teaching neglects the contextual variables of the classroom, it fails to adopt and incorporate the funds of knowledge (González, Moll, & Amanti, 2006) that students (and teachers) bring to the classroom and/or to connect these funds with curricula and instruction. Ultimately, the dominant use of transmission teaching significantly contributes to the reproduction of scholastic inequalities endured by low income and diverse students and serves to uphold the status quo of power imbalances in US society. However, even within the striated system of schooling overcoded and overloaded with molar lines, many educators have long been seeking lines of flight (opportunities to break away from these molar mechanisms) through constructivist pedagogies of social justice, which are taught in many institutions of teacher education today (Cochran-Smith & Villegas, 2016). Despite this focus in teacher education programs, much of the research on first year teaching indicates that teachers' molecular activity—their day-to-day work—tends to return to traditional methods of teaching, which uphold molar agendas (like testing) and perpetuate social inequality. That is, although they may have been exposed to learner-centered, social justice and equity-oriented pedagogies in their preservice learning, first-year teachers struggle to "transfer" this body of knowledge from the university context into their classrooms. In this chapter, we first provide a pedagogical framing for our study by describing dominant pedagogies and teaching for social justice. We then turn to an overview of the challenges first year teachers face in implementing socially just teaching methods in schools.

DOMINANT PEDAGOGIES

Transmission teaching—also known as lecture, direct instruction, teacher-led instruction, or direct transmission—has been the dominant form of instruction for millennia (Cohen, 1988). This type of instruction positions the teacher as teller, as a provider of information, or a filler of an empty receptacle (the student). Described by Freire (1970) as the "banking method" of education, in transmission instruction the teacher is the expert/authority who imparts knowledge as "truth" to passive students. In this model of teaching, the instructional act consists of a one-way transaction of transmitting knowledge to students. Thus, students learn by receiving "deposits" of knowledge from the teacher, and knowledge is defined as previously recorded information that students are expected to memorize. This teaching method has social, cultural, and pedagogical implications, which we summarize below.

From a sociological perspective, transmission teaching is a means by which to indoctrinate and control the population, preserving an asymmetrical balance of power relations in society that ensures an elite few (the privileged or the bourgeoisie) retain control over the masses (the oppressed or the proletariat). By indoctrinating students to learn as passive receivers of knowledge rather than as actively questioning consumers of information, the privileged retain their power: "Translated into practice, this concept is well suited to the oppressors, whose tranquility rests upon how well men fit the world that the oppressors have created, and how little they question it" (Friere, 1970, p. 63). Through both formal and informal (or "hidden") curriculum, youth are inculcated with the ideologies of the dominant culture, and learn to be obedient and quiet (Apple & Beane, 1995). Students are intellectually ranked and segregated, learning to see the world as such, which keeps the populations of the oppressed from understanding the world holistically, and beyond the assumed and internalized paradigm of the privileged, failing to recognize the capacity to join together in solidarity to collectively question hegemonic structures and work to interrupt them (Freire, 1970).

Dominant pedagogies also determine the distribution of cultural capital, or the non-tangible resources that provide privileges to those who possess them (Bourdieu, 1977). Examples of cultural capital in schools include students' conversance with the language of instruction, or "academic English," and background knowledge of the dominant culture on which success in schooling is predicated. Because the language of school is based on dominant ideology and culture, students who arrive with linguistic and cultural resources or funds of knowledge that differ from those valued in school settings enter with a disadvantage. These students are unable to reap the full benefits of schooling because they do not possess the cultural capital necessary for academic success. In other words, only students who are already familiar with the language and culture of schooling are likely to be successful, as Bourdieu (1973) explains:

An educational system which puts into practice an implicit pedagogical action, requiring initial familiarity with the dominant culture, and which proceeds by imperceptible familiarization, offers information and training which can be received only by subjects endowed with the system of predispositions that is the condition for the success of transmission and of the inculcation of the culture. (p. 80)

If non-mainstream students are provided instruction based on pre-packaged information that they are expected to assimilate whole, as transmission teaching does, they will struggle to engage with and make sense of the learning experiences in which they are expected to participate and the academic content they are expected to master. These conditions serve to further hinder their chances of success in school by diminishing the capacity to learn the language of school and/or academic content, and ultimately these students may become disengaged with their education. Because students from more affluent (the dominant or mainstream) backgrounds are more likely to already enter school with this "initial familiarity," they have no need to learn and acquire this cultural capital and thus they are accordingly positioned for academic success. Those students who are not (and are not provided appropriate supports to learn the dominant discourse of school) most likely face failure. As educational attainment is tightly connected to life success, this pattern then results in the reproduction of socio-economic class status and the maintenance and expansion of inequalities present in society (Bourdieu, 1973).

Yet, despite the pervasiveness of the transmission model in schools historically and today, scholars and teacher educations have theorized, researched, and presented alternative approaches to teaching and learning for decades. From a pedagogical perspective, transmission teaching conflicts with the social constructivist/ sociocultural views of how students learn that are currently recognized within educational circles and taught in preservice institutions (e.g., Black & Ammon, 1992; Villegas & Lucas, 2002; Cochran-Smith, 2004; Vygotsky, 1978; Windshitl, 2002). In teacher education programs, generally teacher candidates learn that students do not make meaning by osmosis, but rather by actively working with ideas through social interaction. Traditional transmission teaching also contradicts the understanding that powerful learning happens ecologically, with curriculum functioning as "interacting constituent elements of the whole" (Freire, 1970, p. 95). Rather than facilitating learning as connected wholes, the traditional transmission structure of instruction promotes a fragmented vision of reality by dividing subjects into discrete disciplines, breaking knowledge into discrete bits of information, and separating conceptual and procedural learning (Dewey, 1938). In this model, students receive pre-packaged information absent of any critical inquiry, higher order thinking, synthesis, and/or integration of content with self and community—ensuring that they work to fit into the world as it exists rather than recognize their role as active constructors of their own understanding of, and role in, the world (Dewey, 1938; Freire, 1970/1998).

TEACHING FOR SOCIAL JUSTICE

For over a hundred years, educators and philosophers of education have argued for a shift in teaching practices that moves away from the transmission method. Throughout the twentieth century, scholars have generated a rich body of theory and research articulating conceptions of teaching differently, both to shift the learning experience away from transmission methods and as a form of resistance to education's role in the reproduction of socioeconomic and cultural inequality. These ideas contributed to the emergence of the social justice in education movement (Zeichner, 2003). Below, we discuss our understanding of teaching for social justice, which we see as encompassing three major components: learner centered instruction, responsive and relevant practices, and critical teaching perspectives.

Learner-Centered Instruction

Some scholars have noted that while not all constructivists are social justice educators, all social justice educators are constructivists (e.g., Hinchey, 1998; Villegas & Lucas, 2002). The same principle applies for learner-centered instruction, which is informed by constructivist views. We argue that teaching informed by social justice should have at its foundation constructivist views of knowledge and learning, which should guide learner-centered pedagogy.

Traditional transmission methods are rooted in a positivistic epistemology—that is, the belief that there is one objective truth, "right" ways of thinking, and bodies of knowledge that are "correct" (Giroux, 2002). Social justice educators critique positivism for its obfuscation of the value-based, constructed nature of knowledge and, in turn, its privileging of certain ways of knowing/knowledge in schools while marginalizing others. From a rhizomatic perspective, transmission models and the underlining orientation toward positivism reflect arborescent thought and ways of being. In contrast, the spectrum of constructivist learning theories, as their names suggest, recognize the collaboratively constructed nature of knowledge and learning processes. Because of their insistence that knowledge is created, rather than existing out there already, constructivist perspectives problematize rational views of knowledge as objective/neutral and create space for the possibility and validation of multiple perspectives, knowledges, and ways of knowing (Belenky, Clinchy, Goldberger, & Tarule, 1983; Hinchey, 1998; Villegas & Lucas, 2002). Thus, a constructivist orientation to teaching and learning aligns more closely with rhizomatic thought and being, as opposed to arborescent, transmission-based approaches. In this book, we adopt a social constructivist or sociocultural learning stance, meaning that knowledge is constructed through mediated interaction with others in a particular time/context (Dewey, 1925; Vygotsky, 1978). In this perspective, learning is a process that requires active participation with teacher or peers in the zone of proximal development, or

> ...the distance between the actual developmental level as determined by independent problem solving and the level of potential development as determined through problem solving under adult guidance or in collaboration with more capable peers. (Vygotsky, 1978, p. 84)

Thus, instruction undergirded by a social constructivist theory of learning means that learning is best accomplished through the collaborative and active participation of learners. This type of learner-centered pedagogy supports social justice in multiple ways. For one, adopting the view that knowledge is constructed by individuals allows the teacher to tap into diverse students' resources, or cultural capital, to facilitate their meaning-making of instructional content. By so doing, she provides both access to the dominant curriculum that traditionally excludes these students as well as personally relevant and culturally meaningful lessons. learner-centered pedagogy also builds students' understanding of their role as active meaning-makers/constructors in their academic experiences, which assists them in developing an agentic (rather than passive) stance toward learning. This orientation, in turn, helps them become independent, critical thinkers and active participants in their learning instead of being positioned as powerless victims in society (Villegas & Lucas, 2002).

To be sure, social constructivism is a productive, even emancipatory learning theory. However, it is not a theory of *teaching*. Thus, we employ inquiry-based instruction as a useful theoretical frame regarding teaching that is well suited and aligned with social constructivism. In inquiry-based teaching, curriculum is tied to problem-posing, which involves cycles of investigation, joint dialogue, and reflection between teacher and students. Although inquiry-based instruction may be structured or unstructured and occur on a continuum between teacher- and student-led lessons and activities, students are generally positioned as agents who ask and investigate questions that are relevant and of personal interest. This frame, then, troubles the traditional binary of "teacher/student" and the associated power roles in the classroom. Freire (1970) explains the process as follows: "The teacher is no longer the one who teaches, but one who is himself taught in dialogue with the students, who in turn while being taught also teach. They become responsible for a process in which all grow" (p. 57). By adopting inquiry-as-stance (Cochran-Smith & Lytle, 1999) in their teaching, educators can encourage students to investigate and question their world, interrogate their own beliefs, and explore multiple and sometimes contradictory perspectives (Freire, 1970; Freire & Macedo, 1987).

In some respects, inquiry-based learning often follows a cycle that approximates the scientific method. A typical inquiry cycle might begin with questioning or problem posing (by teacher or students), followed by an investigation of the question or problem, creation or synthesis from investigative results, sharing and discussing the synthesis, and reflection on the process (perhaps to be followed by revising the question and beginning the cycle anew) (Bruner, 1965). Others present a variation on this cycle that perhaps might begin with a "wondering and wandering" phase to spark a question or investigative impetus (Short, Harste, & Burke, 1989; Taylor & Otinsky, 2007) or suggest that problem posing, investigation, and dialogue produce particular actions on the part of students (Freire, 1970). These recursive cycles or spirals of investigation, dialogue, and reflection/action lead to the practice of *education as freedom* as students become increasingly agentic in their learning:

> Students, as they are increasingly posed with problems relating to themselves
> in the world and with the world, will feel increasingly challenged and obliged

15

to respond to that challenge…their response to the challenge evokes new challenges, followed by new understandings; and gradually the students come to regard themselves as committed. (p. 57)

Culturally and Linguistically Responsive Teaching

A second strand of teaching for social justice includes responsiveness to student cultural and linguistic diversity. In the past few decades, the US has experienced dramatic demographic transformations that have led to historic numbers of linguistically and culturally diverse students enrolling in K-12 schools (Lucas, 2011). As mentioned previously, students from mainstream US backgrounds already come to school possessing valued cultural and linguistic capital, which is needed to access school knowledge. As a result, students who do not come from the power majority (white, middle class or affluent) often score lower on standardized academic assessments when compared to their mainstream peers. The so-called "achievement gap" has led to what some researchers (e.g., Banks et al., 2005) have deemed a *demographic imperative*—that is, we must improve the educational access and quality afforded to diverse student populations. Part of this imperative includes ensuring teachers can provide instruction that responds to the particular cultural, linguistic, academic, and social needs of different groups of students (Cochran-Smith, 2004; Villegas & Lucas, 2007; Ladson-Billings, 1995).

Grounded in anthropological theories of "cultural mismatch" at school (Villegas, 1988) and critiques of a "one size fits all" diversity approach categorizing all cultures under the umbrella "other" (Nieto, 2000), culturally responsive instruction emphasizes teaching students by tapping into their cultural backgrounds, their personal, familial and community resources, and academic abilities. This type of pedagogy involves teachers actively working to close the gap between students' home and school lives. To work toward this aim, teachers must "gain knowledge of the cultures represented in their classrooms, then translate this knowledge into instructional practice" (Villegas, 1991, p. 13). Culturally responsive pedagogy includes actively infusing multiple perspectives into lessons/ curricula, using knowledge of students' backgrounds and cultural resources to create bridges to content, and engaging families in their children's education (Villegas & Lucas, 2002).

Another response to the aforementioned demographic imperative, linguistically responsive instruction (Lucas, Villegas, & Freedson-Gonzales, 2008; Lucas & Villegas, 2013), is pedagogy that includes a set of affirmative teacher orientations, skills, and knowledge for teaching ELs and other linguistically diverse students. Rooted in sociolinguistic perspectives (Vygotsky, 1978; Lantolf & Thorne, 2006) and understandings of language as cultural capital, this type of pedagogy advocates for all teachers to learn how language develops, and how to support that development in mainstream classrooms. According to Villegas and Lucas (2011), linguistically responsive teachers have particular beliefs and attitudes toward teaching multi-lingual learners, including consciousness of the sociopolitical aspects of language learning, value for diversity, and willingness to advocate on behalf of their language learner students. Necessary skills and knowledge for linguistically responsive pedagogy include the ability to gain knowledge of their students' backgrounds and resources, key understandings of second language acquisition, and the ability to create supports for their students to access linguistically challenging content. Central to this pedagogy is providing opportunities to practice speaking, reading, and writing the language with appropriate scaffolds (Gibbons, 2002), ensuring that activities are inclusive of all learners (Villegas, Lucas, & Freedson-Gonzales, 2008), and explicitly valuing students' heritage languages (L1) to both foster positive identity and help students transfer skills they may have already learned in their L1 (Cummins, 2000).

Building relationships with students and families is also an important piece of culturally and linguistically responsive pedagogy (Cochran-Smith, 2004; Delpit, 1988; Ladson-Billings, 1994; Villegas & Lucas, 2002). Engaging with families of students helps teachers gain understandings about different facets of their students' lives, which in turn facilitates the connections teachers must make between students home cultures/languages and those of schooling to increase their chances of academic success. Further, building relationships with students is an important, but often overlooked aspect of responsive teaching. While traditional discourses of schooling tend to isolate intellectual activities from affective ones (Zembylas, 2007), some researchers have argued that personal connections in the classroom tend to influence or motivate historically marginalized populations of students more than academic achievement in and of itself (e.g., Delpit, 2006). Because the cultural capital students from non-mainstream backgrounds bring to school tends to be devalued, developing personal relationships with students can help them build a positive self-image and mediate the mismatch they may experience between their home and school lives. As Villegas and Lucas (2002) note, "The interest of teachers who take the time to know about students from oppressed groups can provide some connectedness to school that they may not feel" (p. 80).

Critical Perspectives

Critical perspectives about the world and systems of education necessarily undergird and infuse pedagogies of social justice. Teachers who seek to enact socially just teaching must develop an inquiry-oriented stance to question dominant structures, ideologies, and culture, as well as understandings of the way systems of schooling and traditional teaching methods reproduce and expand societal inequalities (Freire, 1970; Cochran-Smith, 2004; Giroux, 2002; Villegas & Lucas, 2002). A critical mindset helps teachers understand that teaching is a political act (Cochran-Smith, 2004). By virtue of their practices, they themselves have the potential to actively or passively play a role in the continuing marginalization of children of color, high poverty students, or ELs—or conversely, they can resist and subvert it. From a rhizomatic lens, they can support the molar through their molecular, day-to-day activity, or interrupt the status quo through lines of flight.

One part of a critical mindset includes the development of sociocultural consciousness (Villegas & Lucas, 2002), or the understanding that there are multiple worldviews, and the way one sees the world very much depends on her particular background and other factors (gender, race, class, language, and so on). This involves the recognition that some worldviews are privileged over others, while some are ignored entirely. Another aspect of sociocultural consciousness involves the problematizing of concepts like "meritocracy." Armed with the insight that systems of education fail to provide equal access to the benefits of school for all students, but rather actively discriminate based on students' income levels and possession of valued language/behavior of schooling, teachers can tailor their instruction to diminish or eradicate these gaps in the educational experiences offered to historically underserved populations.

While teachers may not be able to directly affect institutional devices for reproducing societal inequalities—such as tracking students into lower or higher-level classes—they can mediate those structures that appear in their classrooms, such as school discourse and curriculum. The language and culture of schooling, for example, is a powerful exclusionary mechanism that teachers can mediate by explicitly teaching students the "codes" or "rules" by which it operates (Delpit, 2006; Ladson-Billings, 1994; Schleppegrell, 2004). Importantly, we do not advocate for students to give up their cultural norms, heritage languages, or the varieties of English connected to their communities—these are important and valuable resources and are tightly connected to the development of healthy identities and conceptions of self. Instead, we suggest that by becoming conversant with the dominant language and culture of schooling, diverse students are provided access to particular forms of cultural capital, which gives them power in situations where they are often victims. To learn the culture of power in schooling, however, students need direct support to understand and practice educationally valued ways of acting, speaking, and thinking. The teacher's role in doing so is to examine lessons and classroom activities for hidden assumptions about prior knowledge students might have, and ensure they support students to gain that knowledge. For instance, Schleppegrell (2004) argues that one of the implicit expectations of schooling is that students know how to linguistically construct a definition of a term—although that structure is almost never taught. Thus, teachers should ensure that all students understand that, in an academic context, when a definition is required, there is a particular text structure through which it is communicated: A (term) is (explanation) (e.g., a *definition* is an *explanation of meaning*).

A final aspect of social justice pedagogy includes the direct infusion of issues of social justice into classroom lessons. Providing opportunities for students (mainstream and diverse) to investigate issues of social justice can help students themselves develop consciousness about inequalities and probe ideas about the contribution of social and institutional structures to historical and current oppressions (Freire, 1970).

This investigation and dialogue should not only help marginalized and mainstream students become more reflective about societal injustices, but also to "talk back to the world" and become agents of change in their own lives (Au, Bigelow, & Karp, 2007, p. xi). Such critical teaching practice might involve students critiquing the relevance of their curriculum (Schultz, 2008) or investigating and analyzing relevant issues from their personal lives or community (Grant, 2012). Alongside providing opportunities to critically question, explore, and act upon issues of social justice, an equity-minded teacher should also model activism (Cochran-Smith, 2004) or change agency (Achinstein & Ogawa, 2011; Villegas & Lucas, 2002) for her students.

CHALLENGING THE STATUS QUO AS A FIRST YEAR TEACHER

Many teacher preparation programs have focused on variations of teaching for social justice either explicitly (e.g., Cochran-Smith et al., 2009) or through promotion of progressive pedagogies (e.g., Black & Ammon, 1992; Cochran-Smith & Villegas, 2016). Yet the body of research investigating the practices of first-year teachers generally shows that, despite being prepared in more socially-just and/or learner-centered ways, they generally tend to adopt practices consistent with transmission teaching and authoritarian classroom management methods (e.g., Allen, 2009; Stanulis, Fallona, & Pearson, 2002). On a closer examination of the literature, we can see that new teachers must navigate multiple, simultaneous elements in their first year settings, including themselves, in the particular assemblages in which they are embedded. That is, teachers are multiplicities (their own beliefs, backgrounds, education) within multiplicities (the classroom, larger school, district, so on), and the way the particular elements of these multiplicities come together shapes the practices she is able to enact.

The Teacher Multiplicity

Teachers bring multiple elements to their teaching that factor into the practices that emerge in their first year of instruction, including knowledge gained in preservice teacher preparation (Allen, 2009; Beck, Kosnik, & Rowsell, 2007; Bianchini & Cazavos, 2007; Chubbock, 2008; Hargreaves & Jacka, 1995; Fry, 2007; Massengil, Mahlios, & Barry, 2005; Tait, 2008), beliefs about students and teaching (Bergeron, 2008; Birrell, 1995; Starkey, 2010), and their background experiences (Birrell, 1995; McAlpine & Crago, 1995; Newman, 2010). For example, Brashier and Norris (2007), investigating beginning teachers' implementation of developmentally appropriate curriculum in the early grades, found that many of the first year teachers they studied were aware of the benefits of play and centers and wanted to implement these strategies, which were a central focus of their preservice preparation. However, other factors, such as testing pressures and students' tendencies to become raucous during center time and play opportunities, made teachers conflicted about enacting these practices. In response to this tension, most confessed that they cut out these activities.

Teachers bring beliefs about students and teaching to their practice which also factor into the teaching that is enacted. For example, Starkey (2010) examined the extent to which six high school teachers in New Zealand integrated technology into their instruction. One of the teachers in particular illustrates the potential for traditional beliefs to shape practice. He noted that he used technology in mathematics far less than his colleagues because he believed math was best learned when students could work problems by hand, with paper and a pencil. This belief, interacting with a lack of experience and confidence using technology in math, produced practices that underemphasized technology in this content area.

Teachers' background and life experiences also are influences, as illustrated by studies by McAlpine and Crago (1995) and Birrell (1995). In these two case studies of white teachers teaching diverse student populations (Aboriginal and African-American, respectively), the two teachers struggled to understand the cultures of their students and work with them in productive ways. Eventually, they adopted management practices that were more consistent with their own White educational backgrounds. In the case of the teacher featured in Birrell's (1995) study, the cultural disconnect was so severe that he requested a transfer to a school where the students had assimilated to mainstream white culture. At his new school, the teacher commented, "I like the black kids here, most of them act white, and they do their schoolwork" (p. 141).

The Classroom Multiplicity

The teacher, and her own multiplicity of elements, also interacts with components of the classroom setting to further shape her practice. Although student-teacher interactions are an understudied topic of the literature in general, studies that have focused on this area have found that student behavior, the ways students respond to teacher instruction, and diversity of student needs are powerful influences on the practices that first-year teachers enact. Many teachers report that student behavior—specifically, being noisy or off-task—influences them to adopt more lecture-based or authoritarian styles of teaching/management (Eldar et al., 2003; He & Cooper, 2011; Hebert & Worthy, 2001; Luft & Roehrig, 2005; Romano, 2008; Saka, Southerland, & Brooks, 2009; Towers, 2010; Ulvik, Smith, & Helleve, 2009). For example, the first-year elementary teacher studied by Hargreaves and Jacka (1995) found herself resorting to behavior modification and other authoritarian practices to address behavior issues, a response that conflicted with her preservice learning about student-centered classroom management. She reflected, "I totally disagree with behavior modification, but I felt I had to do something because my classroom management wasn't working and I couldn't function that way in the classroom" (p. 52).

Students' responses to teachers' practices also play a role in the pedagogy enacted over time (Saka, Southerland, & Brooks, 2009; Stanulis, Fallona, & Pearson, 2002; Tait, 2008; Towers, 2010). Saka, Southerland, and Brooks' (2009) comparative case study of two novice science teachers who had graduated from a preservice program emphasizing inquiry-based instruction illustrates the impact of student response to instruction on novice teacher practice. The first teacher, who had expressed a commitment to both teaching through inquiry and equity at the beginning of the school year, became frustrated with his students, whom he felt were unmotivated and lacking in science content knowledge. He adopted a lecture-based approach, which he believed would better meet his students' content needs and would also allow classroom time to address personal issues with them. Rather than responding positively, his students became more disruptive and disengaged. By the end of the year, the teacher had not only adopted practices that were the antithesis of the pedagogy he had learned in his preservice program, but had also become negative toward students and "came to think that some students simply could not be taught science" (p. 1011).

Another factor affecting instruction includes diverse student populations, encompassing socio-culturally diverse students (Bianchini & Cazavos, 2007; Birrell, 1995; Chubbock, 2008; Hargreaves & Jacka, 1995; He & Cooper, 2011; Hollingsworth, 1992; Kilgore, Ross, & Zbikowski, 1990; McAlpine & Crago, 1995; McDonough, 2009; Saka, Southerland, & Brooks, 2009), English learners (Bergeron, 2008; Farrell, 2003; Luft & Roehrig, 2005; McElhone et al., 2009), and students with special needs (Romano & Gibson, 2006; Scherff, 2008; Tait, 2008). In some of these studies, teachers were aware of the need for differentiation of instruction, but struggled to provide it (Bianchini & Cazavos, 2007; Kilgore, Ross, & Zbikowski, 1990; Luft & Roehrig, 2005; Tait, 2008). Instead, teachers taught to the class norm (Massengill, Mahlios, & Barry, 2005) or lowered curricular rigor for the class as a whole (Bianchini & Cazavos, 2007). In others, they were able to draw on their preservice preparation and other resources to modify their instruction appropriately. Bergeron (2008), for example, described one teacher's multiple efforts to support the language skills of her mainly Spanish-speaking students, which included developing her own Spanish language abilities, maximizing conversational interactions through group work, and creating risk-free opportunities to practice English through paired and choral reading activities.

The School Multiplicity

In the larger school environment, multiple human and non-human elements—such as administrators, colleagues, school culture, and institutional structures—influence new teachers' practices. School leaders, for example, can be a powerful source of support and advocacy, providing teachers with guidance and resources and boosting confidence in instruction (Eldar et al., 2003; Farrell, 2003), especially if the principal also advocates for pedagogy consistent with the values of the new teacher (Bergeron, 2008). However, they can also serve as constraining forces for new teachers, as illustrated by a teacher studied by Scherff (2008). The principal refused to support teachers in disciplinary decisions and pressured them to inflate grades, as the teacher explained: "The administration makes us more like the students every day. The students can talk worse to us with no consequences…these kids know you can't do anything to them. Like if you fail a senior, there's a good chance you're gonna see lawyers" (p. 1323). Another constraining factor included principals with instructional visions that conflicted with those of the new teacher. In Stanulis, Fallona, and Pearson's (2002) case study of three new teachers, one was given a negative evaluation for a lesson using a "writer's workshop" format. When she attempted to discuss the pedagogical differences with her mentor, she was told, "Well, usually they don't like to see novice teachers experimenting. They want to see more structure because they are afraid you can't handle something that is not structured" (p. 77).

New teachers' practices are also affected by their colleagues. Allen (2009) found that fourteen graduates of a progressive teacher education program in Australia tended to emulate their more traditional colleagues rather than implementing the pedagogy learned in their preservice program. Similarly, Chubbock et al. (2001) found that beginning teachers' interactions with veterans at their new schools cut into their confidence regarding their intended instructional methods. As one teacher in the study explained, "…some of the teachers in my department were a little more conservative. I would question my own ideas" (p. 372). The opportunity to collaborate with more open-minded colleagues, however, serves as a support for new teachers, encouraging pedagogical growth and confidence building (Andersson & Andersson, 2008; Bianchini & Cazavos, 2007; Lambson, 2010; Loftstrom & Eisenschmidt, 2008).

The collective pedagogical vision supported by school culture is yet another possible shaping factor of new teachers' instruction. Saka, Southerland, and Brooks's (2009) comparative case study is instructive on this point. Their research suggests that the different experiences of the two teachers—and the degree to which they implemented the inquiry-based pedagogy of their preservice programs—were related in large part to the school cultures. One teacher taught in a school that was labeled as failing under No Child Left Behind, and as a result had adopted a culture that emphasized testing, privileged rote teaching methods, and promoted an individualistic mentality among teachers. Although the teacher initially attempted to implement inquiry-based lessons, the combination of the school culture and his challenging student behavior influenced his adoption of traditional, lecture-based pedagogy. In contrast, his fellow graduate took a job with a school that was recognized for its high achievement. The school collectively valued a constructivist paradigm, which was consistent with beliefs formed during preservice learning, and the collaborative organizational culture supported his interactions with teachers who reinforced an inquiry-based pedagogy. In addition, his students were a more homogenous and well-behaved group who responded positively to inquiry-based teaching practices. Not surprisingly, the researchers reported that the teaching of the second teacher mirrored the reform-based pedagogy learned in his teacher preparation program. Allen (2009) concurs, "novitiates struggle to provide change agency within the school environment unless the community within which they work supports their attempts" (p. 653).

School structures, such as the type of teaching assignment given to new teachers, also factors into the production of teaching practice (Farrell, 2003; He & Cooper, 2011; Kilgore, Ross, & Zbikowski, 1990; Romano, 2008; Stanulis, Fallona, & Pearson, 2002; Starkey, 2010; Tait, 2008). Despite being new to the profession, beginning teachers often receive the most difficult teaching assignments, which is echoed by studies that cite teachers' classroom management concerns and the wide diversity of student needs, cultures, and languages that new teachers encounter—all of which constrain teachers' ability to teach in progressive ways. Describing the challenging assignments beginning teachers often received, Tait (2008) explains:

New teachers get the difficult kids that no one wants to teach. They get the split classes, they get the portables...when you look at the business community, you'd never think of starting someone new off with that many strikes against them. And they wonder why people quit after five years. (p. 12)

Reiterating this point, a new teacher who left the profession after her first year reflected, "I shouldn't have been given the worst classes...[I was] thrown to the wolves" (Scherff, 2008, p. 1327).

The District, State, and Federal Multiplicities

Most of the interactions shaping teaching practice happen in the local environment—the classroom and the school setting, with students and other people, contextual conditions, and so on. Yet larger educational systems also exert powerful influences, such as district, state or federal policies regarding mandated curriculum and standards (Allebone, 2006; Bianchini & Cazavos, 2007; Brashier & Norris, 2008) or accountability and testing (Bergeron, 2008; Romano & Gibson, 2006; Saka, Southerland, & Brooks, 2009; Stanulis, Fallona, & Pearson, 2002). These mandated policies often perpetuate the status quo of teaching. As an illustration, Brashier & Norris found that specific district curriculum emphasizing academic skills and precluding play activities made it less likely that the early elementary teachers in their study would plan and enact instruction that was developmentally appropriate. At the national level, beginning teachers in a study by Allebone (2006) credited a numeracy policy stressing math achievement for their decisions to ability-group students in that subject.

Multiplicities within Multiplicities

Importantly, the influences noted in the sections above do not work in isolation—they occur simultaneously and are productive of particular practices that may be progressive, reinforce the status quo, or comprise a hybrid of practices. Indeed, it is the particular conflux of elements itself—the assemblage in total – and the way they iteratively work together that determines the type of teaching activity that occurs, although one or more elements might exert more influence than others. This is the *molecular work* of teaching-assemblages, the day-to-day collective activity producing particular teaching practices. Bergeron (2008) provides an example of the way multiple elements in a teaching-assemblage might work together. One elementary teacher, who had attended a teacher preparation program that emphasized culturally responsive pedagogy, began teaching at an elementary school with a large Latino/a population. The state had recently passed a law forbidding instruction using students' native languages—which contradicted the principles the teacher had learned in her initial teacher education coursework. However, the principal was a staunch advocate for culturally diverse students, and she encouraged the teacher to pursue bilingual instruction as a support for her students. In addition, plentiful support was available at the school. With her principal's support and the collaboration of her colleagues, Bergeron infused her teaching with both Spanish and English and put her preservice learning to work. Her students responded positively to her instructional efforts, and she gained confidence in her teaching from the affirmative feedback she received from students and her principal. In this case, multiple elements—the teacher herself (including her preservice preparation and own beliefs), elements in the classroom environment (the students, their backgrounds, their instructional needs), elements in the classroom setting (the principal, supportive colleagues) and elements from the larger school setting (the state mandate making it illegal to teach in a foreign language) were interacting to shape the teachers' emerging practices.

In this study, we focus our study at the classroom level, although we do so with full acknowledgement that the teacher, her practice, and her classroom environment are situated within larger educational contexts. Doing so, we argue, can provide richly descriptive information about teacher-multiplicities and the molecular lines of beginning teacher assemblages—that is, the ways that they come into composition with other assemblage elements in their teaching settings. Such data can, in turn, provide insight into the work involved in moving teacher learning from their preservice preparation into their classrooms as they begin their careers.

RHIZOMATIC INQUIRY

INTRODUCTION

In educational research, much empirical and conceptual work is undergirded by dominant ideologies and employs methods that reflect arborescent thinking. That is, these approaches to education research are linear processes that aim to reproduce a series of research steps to find an "objective truth" (St. Pierre, 2011; Martin & Kamberelis, 2013). As such, these mainstream forms of research and their accompanying protocols may be viewed as molar formations that segment and striate research, binding inquiry to an acceptable status quo method, whether quantitative or qualitative, and dictating what forms of empirical and conceptual investigations can be considered "research". To produce research that matters, or indeed, is considered research at all, a researcher must adhere to previously-determined protocols or procedures that are rooted in Enlightenment rationalism and positivist epistemology, and fidelity to this set of rules will produce *valid* or *true* results that correspond to reality. In this way, positivist methods and research protocols (which are molar formations) serve as exclusionary mechanisms, denying any validity or trustworthiness to insights, understandings, or interpretations that emerge from other forms of investigation that do not necessarily conform to pre-set methods. Ultimately, such conditions determine what types of knowledge *count* as true, and what types are disregarded as superfluous, unscholarly, or unreliable.

From a Deleuzian perspective, the world (and the human understanding of the world) is conceived as inherently multiple, shifting and mobile, composed of singularities, and open-ended, with no determined starting or ending point (Deleuze & Guattari, 1987). Thus any research perspective predicated on ontological stability, universals, methodologies that reproduce the same bodies of knowledge, and the capacity to discern an ultimate "truth" *as a given* would be incompatible with a Deluzian lens. In fact, we question if Deleuzian and Deleuzoguattarian concepts are compatible with any articulated qualitative research protocol. By "research protocol," we are referring to a set of steps, that while perhaps not entirely linear, generally entail reading available research literature on the topic, crafting some sort of guiding question(s), adopting a procedure that outlines what data to collect and from whom to gather information about that question, following interpretive guidelines, and finally, sharing the "findings" to a primarily academic audience in some sort of consumable form (e.g., a journal article, a book chapter, a monograph).

Yet, we *do* exist in a stratified academic system overcoded with rules. To produce a book, one must be able to impose order, to organize thoughts and information in particular, conventional ways, to generate a text composed of linear sentences stacked on top of another. Thus, eventually, one presents an interpretation, printed on a piece of paper, which turns the initial research inquiry into a representation—a tracing. Deleuze and Guattari (1987), however, acknowledge that tracings and maps are not dichotomous, but bound up with each other. A tracing must always be put back on the map. Whereas the tracing encapsulates normative research methodologies, mapping encompasses the qualities of the rhizome, drawing from and utilizing these non-normative approaches to construct new forms of knowledge, new and previously unthought interpretations of the world, and new understandings of what it means to *be(come)* and to *do*.

In the following pages, we present an overview of our research methodology, which we liken to Deleuzoguattarian mapping. Our approach is informed by rhizomatics, crystallization, and constructivist grounded theory. Our intention is to discuss these ideas with humility and with the caveat that they do not present a fixed, unchanging, and permanent reality. These bodies of thought instead express *a* reality, a version of reality held still in time by us, the researchers, and necessarily turned into a tracing for the moment to share our constructed themes. We invite you, the reader, to plug into the tracing, to come into composition with it, explore your relations with it, and in doing so, *reactivate* it, and put the tracing back on the map.

THINKING DIFFERENTLY IN RHIZOMATIC RESEARCH

Adopting a rhizomatic approach theoretically and methodologically requires that researchers embrace multiple shifts in thinking about their own inquiry, which carries implications for the way studies are designed, conducted, and reported. In recent decades, the "gold standard" of educational research has reverted to experimental positivist research that demonstrates utilitarian benefit, or "what works" (St. Pierre & Roulston, 2006; St. Pierre, 2011). This type of research produces simplistic accounts of very complex and multifaceted phenomena, such as teaching practice, that are in actuality comprised of contextually situated, historically contingent, and relationally produced processes mitigated through language, material conditions, and previous and anticipated life experiences. Importantly, however, positivist studies underscored by notions of an objective reality and essential truth to be found, "out there," contradicts commonly accepted educational research in the area of pedagogy. While much educational qualitative research continues to follow positivist ideals of research, the reigning theory of knowledge construction, or learning, in the field of education is just that—the idea that *knowledge is constructed* rather than *found whole already existing out there*. If we agree that we construct our understanding of the world, and implicit in that construction is our own selves (and a multiplicity of self/selves at that), it follows that no research we produce can be objective, since we ourselves have constructed it and, therefore, *we as researchers* are bound up in that research. Moreover, since we have constructed it, that knowledge could not have existed previously, "found" somewhere (as we tend to say in reporting our "findings"). In this way, not only do we create research, but the research we make also creates the world (Colman & Ringrose, 2013).

Positivistic research is also undergirded by the understanding that humans are stable, agentic bodies in the world with the capability to produce rational thought (St. Pierre, 2000). This idea, which stems from Descartes ("I think, therefore I am"), has become an ideological staple in western society. It is a fundamental notion that serves as a cornerstone of current neoliberal trends, which celebrate entrepreneurialism, rugged individualism, and the personal pursuit of wealth (Harvey, 2005)—furthering the myth of meritocracy and determining that those who have accumulated wealth have worked hard and deserve to enjoy the fruits of their labor, while those who do not have wealth are lazy and deserve to go hungry or without basic necessities. Such a portrait of an autonomous individual also underscores contemporary views of education. The ideal learner is one who is autonomous—who can "master" requisite understandings and competencies and demonstrate them by her/himself. For example, students' assessments are based on their individual performances on standardized achievement tests. Teachers themselves are also considered to be autonomous actors, assumed to be in complete control of their actions and consciously able to "choose" to teach in particular ways.

A rhizomatic perspective shifts from a view of the world as made up of autonomous, isolated individuals with agency and a rational capability to one of connected multiplicity. As humans, we are multiplicities within multiplicities—a combination of physical limbs and features, experiences, desires, beliefs and histories, always in composition with other tangible and intangible elements—that together produce action, power relations, and agency. As an illustration, imagine a teacher sitting at a desk in an empty classroom. From a humanist perspective, the teacher is a separate entity from the desk and the physical space. However, taking up a rhizomatic perspective, the scene could be described as an amalgam of teacher-desk-classroom, together with many other elements. When an element of the assemblage changes, its functioning changes. That is, the multiplicity becomes different. Take time, for instance. The teacher at her desk in her classroom in the morning before her students arrived would work differently than an assemblage with a teacher sitting at her desk in an empty classroom at six o'clock in the evening of the same day. Still different would be the same teacher at her desk in an empty classroom on a Saturday morning.

This view of life as multiple, as assemblage, raises additional issues for most qualitative research, which is also grounded in the humanist understanding that individuals may be studied and their words taken to correspond with a fixed and universal reality. For one, we suggest that research foci must move from analyzing the *participant(s)* as individual subjects to analyzing *relationships* among assemblages, taking into consideration both the multiplicity of participant and assemblage.

27

Thus, for the current study, we could not isolate the teacher as the unit of analysis. Instead, we focused on the interactions between teacher and other elements of her assemblage.

Moreover, the notion of assemblage also problematizes traditional ideas of the objective, third-party researcher. In this view, the researcher, as an encapsulated body, may act as separate from the research activity or participants, without "contaminating" the data with their own biases, and thus may produce objective research. Yet, we argue, from a rhizomatic standpoint, the researcher is a multiplicity that works together with participant and data multiplicities in particular ways to produce particular analyses that represent *a* reality.

Such a view also complicates the linear, causal logic attributed to teaching processes in positivistic research. Indeed, if teaching is not an action done by an individual teacher to an individual student, but a production arising from the collective functioning of an entire teaching assemblage, it would be impossible to assign a causal relation to the teaching or the learning. Instead, from a rhizomatic view, there are no one-to-one correspondences. There are only multiplicities which serve as quasi-causes (Deleuze, 1990)—that is, they collectively contribute to a production, but their contribution cannot be isolated and analyzed. It is with these notions in mind that we provide a discussion of our own situated mode of inquiry for the current study, which we turn to next.

POST-QUALITATIVE RESEARCH AND CRYSTALLIZATION

Following researchers who recognize that qualitative research is often still undergirded by positivist notions like objectivity and universality (e.g., Mazzei & Youngblood-Jackson, 2012; MacLure, 2013), we ground this study in a *post-qualitative* paradigm (Lather & St. Pierre, 2013). Expressing both a break with traditional qualitative research and a positioning in the *post* perspectives, post-qualitative research seeks to interrogate and "open up" the taken-for granted notions of traditional research methods (St. Pierre, 2011)—for example, the ideas that there are knowing, autonomous subjects/participants, that the researcher is separate from the study, or that truth or understanding may be "found" in data. As such, post-qualitative research is consistent with a rhizomatic focus on disrupting normalized thinking (in research) and pursuing a non-linear ontology (Strom, 2015).

St. Pierre (2011) warns that post-qualitative research does not offer "a recipe, an outline, a structure…another handy 'research design' in which one can safely secure oneself and one's work" (p. 613). With this in mind, we turned to crystallization (Ellingson, 2009) to provide guiding insights as we forged a nomadic methodological path. Crystallization was originally offered as a postmodern alternative to "validating" qualitative analyses by Richardson (1994), who contended, "…in postmodern mixed-genre texts, we do not triangulate; we *crystallize*. We recognize that there are far more than 'three sides' with which to approach the world" (p. 934, original emphasis). Ellingson (2009) expanded this concept, defining crystallization as a methodological framework that

> … combines multiple forms of analysis and multiple genres of representation into a coherent text or series of related texts, building a rich and openly partial account of a phenomenon that problematizes its own construction, highlights researchers' vulnerabilities and positionality, makes claims about socially constructed meanings, and reveals the indeterminacy of knowledge claims even as it makes them. (p. 6)

Crystallization builds on critical, alternative research traditions, such as creative analytic practice (CAP) ethnography (Richardson, 1994) and bricolage (Kincheloe, 2001/2005). These modes of inquiry seek to push beyond traditional qualitative research boundaries by mixing scientific and artistic research genres. Ellingson (2009) outlines the general criteria for crystallized research projects, which she suggests (1) include richly described, complex renderings and interpretations of phenomena; (2) utilize multiple, contrasting methods of knowledge production among genres of qualitative research, including both constructivist and creative approaches; (3) offer multiple modes of textual and visual expression; (4) contain extensive interrogation of the role of the researcher; and (5) regard knowledge as "situated, partial, constructed, multiple, embodied, and enmeshed in power relations" (p. 10). This methodology offered multiple benefits for our study, including guidance for expressing phenomena in a more complex and richly described way, crafting multi-faceted accounts and analyses, and bridging the creative-scientific divide (Ibid). By connecting insights from postmodern frames and multiple points and genres along the qualitative spectrum, crystallization enables the problematizing of dominant methods of inquiry while maintaining a pragmatic focus on contributing understandings regarding practice, research, theory, and/or policy. In this way, such a method avoids the "deconstructionist dilemma" (p. 10), or being immobilized by virtue of critique.

For us as researchers, it also offered us a chance to explore a question we posed to ourselves alongside our examination of *becoming-teacher,* inspired by Deleuze and Guattari's (1987) reference of a Spinozan query, "What can a body do?" (p. 256). We asked ourselves, *"What can a [researcher] do?"* We began the study dissatisfied with qualitative methods that mimic the goals of positivism, yet initial explorations into more "experimental" methods like rhizoanalysis (a more detailed explanation of which is given later in this section) were not satisfying either. As we researched more about crystallization, we realized that this concept would allow us to push not only the boundaries of traditional qualitative methods, but also our own boundaries as researchers. By simultaneously employing and interrogating multiple, systematic methods of research, we could explore the data-rhizome from many different angles. We connected heterogenous pieces of theory and method to one another, putting them in dialogue with one another, creating—and simultaneously ourselves becoming part of—a research assemblage that included rhizomatics, crystallization, case study, and constructivist grounded theory analysis.

CASE STUDY

While crystallization served as a methodological guide, we decided that on a practical level, we would create multiple case studies (Yin, 2009), which complement in-depth investigation into the complicated set of institutional, political, developmental, and personal factors that shape actions in schools and classrooms (Stake, 1995). While other research genres, both qualitative and quantitative, tend to focus on isolating phenomena for further investigation, case study methods allow the researcher to gain a more textured and holistic understanding of complex phenomena that involve multiple interacting elements (Merriam, 1998). Miles and Huberman (1994) refer to a case as "phenomenon of some sort occurring in a bounded context" (p. 25), presenting a visual of a heart inside a circle: the phenomenon under investigation is the heart of the research, and the circle bounds the area of study. Without a rhizomatic frame, in each of the three cases, either the teacher or the practices produced would be the unit of analysis. However, with a multiplistic frame informed by Deleuze and Guattari, our focus shifted to the relations between assemblage elements—both human and nonhuman. The classroom served as the boundary of each case, which allowed the conceptualizing of the teaching-assemblage, although we readily admit that these case edges are porous and fluid.

Additionally, while the literature regarding the teaching practices of first-year teachers is relatively thin, the existing studies often focus on teacher activity at the school level, such as professional development or collegial interactions. Very few studies contain thick description of actual instructional practices or information regarding how these practices are negotiated, which means we know little of what happens in the classrooms of first-year teachers regarding instructional interactions. In other words, not much is known about the molecular work of the teacher, or the teacher's day-to-day translation of macro-level rules and discourses to the micro-level, the activity which works to uphold the status quo of traditional patterns of schooling. As Deleuze and Guattari (1987) note, to learn about social change we must pay attention to the micro-level interactions of the social, "the little imitations, oppositions, and inventions constituting an entire realm of subrepresentative matter" (p. 219). Therefore, while we acknowledge that the teacher and classroom are part of a larger organizational system, and these mutually influence the other, we focused on interactions and relationships between the teacher and other multiplicities of the classroom setting.

THE NORTHEASTERN TEACHER RESIDENCY PROGRAM

All three participants in this study were graduates of the Northeastern Urban Teaching Residency (NUTR). The program mirrors, in part, the urban teaching residency model (Berry, Montgomery, & Snyder, 2008), featuring a year-long apprenticeship in an urban school accompanied by teacher education coursework. However, several unique features distinguish this program from other residencies, including a deeply collaborative and equal-status partnership between a university and school district, a philosophical grounding emphasizing equitable power relations between stakeholders, extremely rigorous admission criteria, a focus on social justice and inquiry-based teaching, and a strong community education component. Because of these unique features, which are not typically characteristic of an urban teacher residency, we deliberately refer to the program as an "urban hybrid teacher education program" rather than a residency.

The program was born of a long-standing partnership between a large public university in the northeastern United States and nearby urban school district. The two entities collaborated to create a program to specifically address a major area of shortage in the urban district—quality secondary math and science teachers. During the 12-month period, NUTR participants were paid a $26,000 stipend and tuition, and upon successful completion of the program, residents received a Masters of Arts in Teaching and a full teaching credential. Graduates signed a contract that committed them to three years of teaching in the urban district. Through this program, the university and urban school district hoped to create a sustainable pipeline of math and science teachers prepared to educate youth from the local community. The program specifically screened for applicants who are not only academically strong, but also have certain dispositions, including the ability to collaborate productively, a commitment to teaching urban youth, and persistence and resilience in the face of adversity (Haberman, 1995). To select residents of this high caliber, potential candidates participated in a rigorous, three-day admissions process involving an application review, individual and group interviews, and school-based interactions.

The program is grounded in the notion of creating a "third space" in teacher education (Zeichner, 2010a). Traditionally, university-based teacher education has provided an experience for future teachers that is characterized by various disconnects, with divides between theory and methods coursework, coursework and practical experience, and the faculty supervisor and the collaborating teacher (Grossman et al., 2009). Creation of a third space seeks to realign traditional power relationships (Bhabha, 1994) and create an alternate arena where the roles of the university, school, teacher candidate, and community can be reimagined. In the third space, each stakeholder is considered to have valid and equal knowledge, and each has a voice in the construction of the program. In keeping with the third space realignment foundation, the traditional structures of university-based teacher education are restructured: instead of a separate period of learning and practice, both are encompassed within the one year apprenticeship. The resident learns in and from practice, simultaneously having the opportunity to learn about teaching while experiencing it, debriefing with expert others and peers about their experiences, and reflecting on them. Furthermore, classroom-based mentor teachers are considered to be teacher educators alongside the university faculty members, collaborate in the construction of curriculum, and lead assignments such as the residents' action research. Through the realignment of traditional roles of teacher preparation and a fusing of learning and practice, the NUTR has attempted to bridge the school-university, theory-practice divide. However, a third space is always a utopian endeavor, and is never fully actualized. While the NUTR has gained some ground in their attempt to create a third space, challenges abound, and the process is never easy or finished (Klein, Taylor, Onore, Strom, & Abrams, 2013).

The NUTR is grounded in a constructivist philosophy of learning and seeks to promote a transformative conception of teaching and learning espousing an inquiry based, dialogical, problem-posing pedagogy that positions students as active meaning makers (Freire, 1970). Program faculty provide coursework experiences that model the practices of such inquiry-based teaching as well as allow residents to acquire deep understanding of their own learning processes, learning through the cycles of actively questioning, investigating, acting, dialoguing, reflecting, and modifying. To ensure an educational experience that is both tailored to the individual teacher candidate as well as the students of the local community, the curriculum is negotiated and continually co-constructed by faculty and residents. Additionally, the relational element of teaching is stressed, with emphasis placed upon community, collaboration, support, and the power of human relationships and personal empathy. When possible, residents are placed in schools, both during their residency and during their three-year term of service, in cohorts of two or more.

Another unique feature of the NUTR is the six-week summer internship, during which residents work with three different community partner agencies through the summer months before their teaching apprenticeship begins. Past internships have included teaching at a science-themed museum summer camp; serving as student "relationship managers" with a local program that facilitates student internships in corporate settings; and recruiting and coordinating youth volunteers for a local non-profit's annual talent show. Working in these capacities gives residents an opportunity to get to know the community in which they will be teaching and interact with community youth in an out-of-school setting.

Learning opportunities are structured around the program principles of inquiry, collaboration, reflection, and opportunities to learn in and from practice (Cochran-Smith & Lytle, 1999). To practice the skills of inquiry into teaching and studying one's own students and practice, residents conduct case studies of one English language learner and one special needs student and conduct an action research project focused on a question generated about teaching practice. Another learning tool, instructional rounds, is "an explicit practice designed to bring discussions of instruction directly into the process of school improvement" through the use of "a set of protocols and processes for observing, analyzing, discussing and understanding instruction that can be used to improve student learning" (City, Elmore, Fiarman, & Teitel, 2009, p. 3). A major assignment in the first semester is developing a complete unit plan using backwards design (Wiggins & McTighe, 2005), featuring essential unit questions, and including multiple authentic assessments. In this assignment, residents present one lesson from their unit plan to the group utilizing a tuning protocol (McDonald, Mohr, Dichter, & McDonald, 2003), providing a structured way to disseminate the lesson and receive input from colleagues: one resident presents the lesson, and the group reflects on what they heard, providing constructive feedback.

While engaged in preservice coursework, residents co-teach on a full time basis with a carefully selected mentor teacher. To simulate the first-year teaching experience as closely as possible, residents are expected to participate in the same professional tasks as a full-time teacher of record, including non-instructional tasks such as attending faculty meetings. As often as possible, mentor teachers are assigned two preparation periods to provide time for collaborative planning. NUTR university faculty members observe residents frequently, working with mentors to provide guidance to residents regarding classroom practice.

Community building and collaboration is another important aspect of the program. A multi-layered support network is created for the residents from day one, encompassing not only the mentors and program faculty, but also doctoral students assigned as program assistants, department chairs, other teachers, and science and math faculty from the university. A strong emphasis is also placed on building community within and among the cohort of residents, so that they create their own support network with which to combat the perennial isolation that plagues many new teachers. Induction support is also provided for residents for the first three years of their inservice teaching, with each graduate assigned an induction coach who serves as a general resource and additional layer of support to the resident.

DATA SOURCES AND COLLECTION

As noted above, the participant group included three first-year, secondary science teachers in a large urban school district who were graduates of the NUTR program. Given their common experience in this program, we were interested in the ways that the teachers might negotiate their learning and experiences with their new contexts to construct practice. Although the qualitative methods section typically contains descriptions of the participants and setting or context, we offer those in each participants' corresponding chapter. Below, we describe each of our data sources, which included classroom observations, observation debriefs, semi-structured interviews, field notes, and a researcher journal. These were collected by the lead author over a five-month, one semester period commencing in September, at the start of the school year.

Observations

Because the study focuses on teachers' negotiation of practices in the classroom setting specifically, a key data source of the study was classroom observations.

Observations of classroom activity allowed direct documentation of teacher practices and the viewing of the interactions between teacher and students in a naturalistic setting that, over time, influenced the development of those practices. These observations, then, facilitated a first-hand encounter with the phenomena under study (Merriam, 2009). Observations were conducted as a participant observer (Adler & Adler, 1998), where research activities were made known, but no active role was taken in classroom happenings. However, despite the first author's aim to remain in the background, she was often drawn in to become a part of the fabric of the classroom—that is, she herself became a part of the classroom assemblage, again demonstrating the blurring of boundary between researcher and participants. Students would often approach her to curiously ask, "What are you writing? Are you writing about me?" At times, she even became part of the lesson itself. For example, during a discussion about tectonic plates, Mauro told the class, "Katie is from California, she probably knows all about earthquakes. Katie, have you been in one?" I (Katie) looked up from my laptop in surprise, and found myself telling the students about the last time the earth shook under my feet when I lived in San Diego.

The total number of observations varied for each teacher. Because we were interested in the construction of practice, each teacher was observed for the length of one unit, so that several consecutive lessons that supported a larger learning objective might be documented and analyzed. For June and Mauro, whose classes were eighty-minute periods, this meant seven and five classes were observed, respectively. However, for Bruce, whose classes were only forty minutes, one unit spanned ten classes. In addition to the complete unit, each teacher was observed three times in September to get an understanding of classroom dynamics. Finally, a "mini-unit," which consisted of three classes each, was observed toward the end of the semester to note any additional changes or developments that might have taken place since the observed unit. Because each class is a unique composition of the teacher, students, content, affects, forces, and objects that shapes what the teacher can do, the observation schedule was planned to observe as many different periods as time allowed so multiple "teaching-assemblages" for each participant might be observed.

During each observation, the first author took notes in a method that combines the overview and scripting methods (Acheson & Gall, 1992), alternately capturing what was done and said during the lesson with as much detail as possible. Because the study question focused on the construction of practice, particular attention was given to the teachers' instructional methods and strategies as well as interactions between the teacher and other individuals or elements in the class. For each observation, separate field notes were kept to record the researcher's own thoughts, apart from the script, during the lesson. These field notes included new insights, connections to theory or other data, methodological decisions, or personal reactions to the observation.

After each lesson, the first author conducted a 15–20 minute debrief with the teacher. This "observational debrief" provided an opportunity to informally interview the teacher regarding the process of teaching and the lesson itself. The debrief took place either directly after the lesson was taught or at the conclusion of the school day, as the teacher's schedule allowed. This short, informal interview was critical to capture the in-the-moment thinking that might not be possible for the participant to reconstruct at a later time. The observational debrief was also used as a way to confirm or disconfirm the researcher observations from the particular lesson or probe further on specific topics. As the unit progressed, the information and reflections the teachers provided in the debriefs, together with the observations, helped to focus the emerging connections we were beginning to make with the data, and these were brought to the attention of the teacher as a form of member checking. Each debrief was recorded and transcribed verbatim. These transcripts, along with the observation script and field memos, were used to write a more complete, narrative account of each lesson after each observation.

Interviews

While observations were important to the main research question, interviews were a critical complementary data source. Classroom observations provide only a partial view of teaching. Planning and other preparation for instruction, teacher beliefs and background, and factors from outside the classroom—such as testing pressures, school policies, or school structures—also influence the process of teaching that occurs in class. Interviewing participants provided a window into teacher thinking and other teaching-assemblage elements that might not have been apparent in observations but are essential for constructing an understanding of the ongoing process of negotiating teacher practices. Further, from a methodological standpoint, discussing the practices and interactions recorded with teachers is essential for trustworthiness and member-checking purposes. During formal interviews, the participants were able to provide clarification, confirmation or disconfirmation, fill in gaps, and/or build on emerging themes or ideas presented about the participants' practices, all of which increase the plausibility of the study.

Two semi-structured interviews (Merriam, 2009) were conducted with each participant, one at the beginning and one toward the end of the semester. The original interview provided a glimpse into the teacher's thinking and perception of her work as she transitioned into the classroom for the first time. We developed a set of open-ended questions prior to the interview, which served as a guide rather than a strict protocol (Patton, 1990). The purpose of the second, and final, interview was to probe the teacher's thinking about her work and her perceived development over the previous several months. This interview was also an opportunity to follow up on themes that were emerging or topics we thought would be fruitful as the data collection neared its conclusion. This second interview was also critical for presenting emerging "findings" to the participants for their feedback, which helped us align our ideas with the understandings of our participants. Each interview was approximately 60–90 minutes and was audio-recorded and transcribed verbatim.

ANALYSIS

Although our analytic process was inductive and we refer to the ideas presented through our constructed cases as "findings," we do so only to render them as recognizable to readers, as we "found" nothing in the data. Rather, the data are immanent, containing no higher transcendent truths or fixed reality to be found by us, the researchers. Nor did the themes "emerge," as if they were waiting, fully formed, for us to discover them. Rather, we ourselves imposed boundaries, identified elements that we decided comprised assemblages, theorized relations between these elements, and *constructed* the key ideas from them. To do so, we drew on multiple analytic methods, including constructivist grounded theory methods (Charmaz, 2006; Clarke, 2003), which we found supported our view of teaching as complex social phenomena. Rather than using these analytic procedures as rigid protocols, we drew on them as heuristic strategies (Clarke, 2005) to actively create the understandings by making multiple and recursive connections between and among data sources and empirical and theoretical literature. Below, we describe our analytic process, which itself was non-linear and multiplicitous.

We began with Eakle's (2007) strategy of "data-walking," meadering through data without a map or without codes in mind. As interesting things drew our attention, we highlighted them and made notes. We pulled these interesting tidbits out and began placing them in maps that we created, clustering them around "main ideas" that related to our question. These certainly showed the complexity of the developing practices and the multitude of issues, events, ideas, beliefs, and interactions that came together in each teaching assemblage to shape the development of practice. However, after the construction of a few maps, we realized that we needed to organize the "evidence" for each of the main ideas, which we treated as flexible categories (although not liking the idea of the *category,* we needed some way to contain the data and organize it). While the maps communicated the complexity of the teaching multiplicities to the reader who did not construct them, we worried that by themselves, the maps might look like a jumbled morass of phrases attached to keywords, difficult to navigate at best and at worst, meaningless. Thus we created charts that organized the quotes, snippets of action, and our nascent analysis by keyword or theme.

We then began a second layer of analysis, making notes and further developing key ideas. We still hesitated to call these codes, as we wanted to treat them as fluid and overlapping, and the very word "code" evoked the Deleuzian use of *overcoding*, which refers to the way that molar lines stratify our existence (Deleuze & Guattari, 1987). While some Deleuzian researchers might resist the development of themes, patterns, or tendencies, however, we argue that as long as they are not presented as one single truth or reality, organizing text using themes, main ideas, patterns, and so on can help provide the reader an accessible overview of complex phenomena (Ellingson, 2009). Additionally, contemporary grounded theory "theming" differs from other interpretive qualitative coding, as it focuses on actions and processes rather than topics or things (Charmaz, 2006), which is consistent with a Deleuzian focus on movements and how things work, as well as larger agendas of change for social justice (Charmaz, 2011).

As we began to create themes based on the grounded theory analysis, we noticed they mainly echoed the original ideas we had begun to construct from the initial rhizomatic mapping, reminding us that "all analyses come from particular standpoints, including those emerging in the research process" (Charmaz, 2011, p. 510). Yet, although charting the data according to main ideas created a paper trail for our "evidence," it precluded the drawing of relationships and showing overlapping, leaking pieces of evidence. In other words, it did not necessarily accomplish what the map did in terms of showing the many, many aspects that were simultaneously influencing the development of teacher practice. Furthermore, we became frustrated with the decontextualizing nature of separating sentences from their data source—we felt that this process leached out the complexity, the messiness, and contextual uniqueness that we wanted to convey to the reader.

From here, we began our third "level" of analysis. As we pulled evidence to map and plot into the charts, we also began to write analytic memos (Charmaz, 2006) that contained lengthier descriptions of events, connecting across data sources—annotated memos, the observation scripts, the debrief interviews, and the formal interviews—to begin to form coherent "data stories" or narratives. We took each of these stories and plotted them on an overarching map, using the charts to identify pieces of evidence specific to these stories and create a record of evidence for each story or idea. During this process, we continued to generate new connections that had not occurred to us as we crafted the initial maps, and we iteratively returned to the maps to plot these new linkages. Thus, putting these two methods in dialogue with each other allowed us to explore the data in multifaceted ways (Ellingson, 2009).

Using our memos, maps, and other analytic tools, we began assembling the cases, which we present in the subsequent three chapters. We constructed narratives, because, following Ellingson (2009), we believe "Narratives constructed from fieldnotes, interview transcripts, or other data enable the reader to think with and feel with a story, rather than only analyzing its meaning…narratives enable qualitative researchers to show rather than tell" (p. 65). The case studies are presented with an interwoven combination of ethnographic narrative, as well as the products of our constructivist grounded theory analysis and "thinking with" rhizomatics. Together, we suggest, these methods crystallize into a more coherent and complex description of the negotiation of first year teaching practice.

ETHICS AND TRUSTWORTHINESS

One of the attractions of the multiple frames we used (both of crystallization and rhizomatics in particular) is the nod to the creative power of the researcher. On the one hand, we hope that readers consider our study of teacher becomings to be trustworthy from our efforts to convey transparency, the use of multi-method crystallization itself, and strategies such as ongoing member checks. However, we also state upfront that this research is a construction by us, influenced and rendered partially by virtue of our positionalities, research orientations, and social justice agendas. We acknowledge and continually remind ourselves that this text is our creation. It was designed based on our interests, passions, beliefs, and values. Observations were conducted with an eye that focused on the question of practice construction with a foregrounding in social justice and interviews were guided by the study focus, which again was informed by our particular interests. We sifted through the data, marking items that seemed interesting or relevant to the question we had chosen, and we chose data stories that we hoped would be exemplars to illustrate the complexities of enacting social-justice focused practice. With this in mind, we also employed a number of strategies to attempt to create as transparent, multiplicitous, and rigorous a study as possible to convince the reader and academic community of the plausibility and relevance of this work.

The notion of validity, as traditionally characterized by academic research, speaks to the legitimation of generated knowledge (Lather, 1993). Because the purpose of this study is not to necessarily generate knowledge, but rather to produce thinking, the concept of trustworthiness—the argument that a study's findings are "worth paying attention to" (Lincoln & Guba, 1985, p. 290)—is more suited to our intentions than validity for demonstrating that the research is rigorous, authentic, and contributes to understanding. This last criteria of "understanding" is particularly important because our study, in the Deleuzian tradition, fundamentally seeks to investigate the question of "How does it work?" in relation to first-year teaching practice.

Issues of trustworthiness are, at their heart, issues of quality. Rather than asking if a study's findings match reality or can be reproduced exactly, trustworthiness seeks to establish credibility and plausibility (Merriam, 2009). Strategies of triangulation (Mathieson, 1988) are a common approach to increasing a study's trustworthiness. The term *triangulation*, however, implies a notion of the fixed points and rigidity that seems contradictory to a research study with postmodernist sensibilities. Instead of triangulating between points, we again turn to the overarching frame of crystallization, which, as a way to confirm the plausibility of our analytic constructions, aligns with the ideas of multiplicities invoked by the rhizome and of the multiple subject positions that necessarily influence this research. Richardson (1994) notes, "Crystals are prisms that reflect externalities and refract within themselves, creating different colors, patterns, and arrays casting off in different directions. What we see depends on our angle of repose—not triangulation but rather crystallization" (p. 963). To this end, we designed the study to provide multiple opportunities for crystallization at every stage of research, linking and searching for commonalities or confirmation of findings among and between interviews, field notes, observation scripts, and debriefs. The inclusion of multiple cases also offer an opportunity for crystallization—as Miles and Huberman (1994) note, " By looking at a range of similar and contrasting cases, we can understand a single case finding, grounding it by specifying *how* and *where* and, if possible, *why* it carries on as it does" (p. 29). Additionally, we present findings in narrative, thickly descriptive case studies that provide a different view of connections, ideas, and stories in each case, allowing readers to evaluate whether the study findings are transferrable to their own contexts.

Katie's Positionality

My identities as educational activist, former urban teacher, and teacher educator-researcher have spurred my interest in this study, shaped its design, and informed its evolution. My experiences as an urban educator and school leader draw me to research regarding quality, effective pathways to urban teaching as well as fuel my commitment to research and teaching that will lead to broader, societal change addressing culturally sanctioned, institutionalized racism, sexism, and classism. Furthermore, my political beliefs, including my resistance to encroaching market-based reforms that adopt simplistic, linear formulas to evaluate teaching and learning, has led me to seek different epistemologies, conceptual frameworks, and research methods that can account for the unpredictability and non-linearity that characterize teaching. These factors contributed to our adoption of a social justice conceptual framework and qualitative methods that include rhizoanalysis.

As a teacher educator and former doctoral fellow, my interest in innovations in urban teacher preparation led to my assignment to the hybrid teacher education program featured in this study as part of my fellowship. As previously noted, I served as an NUTR faculty assistant for two years. I collected data from the program, which included interviewing and observing preservice teachers, including those who participated in this study. I also led supplemental workshops on topics such as content area literacy and classroom management. Additionally, I completed my doctoral practicum as an induction coach for the first three graduates of the program featured in this study, providing mentorship and advocacy during their first year teaching. To address obvious ethical concerns, I stepped out of my role as faculty assistant and induction coach with the NUTR prior to conducting this study, which limited my interactions with research participants outside of my new role as researcher. However, I had pre-existing relationships with all participants, having served in a former capacity as faculty assistant.

Because of these previous relationships with the participants and my history with the program with the program, I am transparent about positioning myself in relation to the research and illuminating the assumptions I bring to the study. To increase the trustworthiness of the study, I embedded member checks into interviews and presented theme constructions to participants throughout the process, incorporating their feedback and expansion on these ideas. We also shared findings with critical friends in an iterative manner (McNiff, Lomax, & Whitehead, 1996). A critical friend is "a trusted person who asks provocative questions, provides data to be examined through another lens, and offers critique of a person's work as a friend" (Costa & Kallick, 1993, p. 50). As someone who has been totally immersed in the NUTR program for the past two years, I relied on my critical friends to play an important role in helping me to mediate my biases as much as possible.

Adrian's Positionality

My identities as a former urban educator and school leader, English-Spanish bilingual, first generation American, and current urban teacher educator compose aspects of my positionality in relation to this study and inform my perspectives on teaching, learning, and education research. As someone who attended P-12 urban schools as a student, and later worked professionally for an urban district, the parallels between myself and the research participants (and their own students) were many. Given my personal and professional experiences with the challenges of urban youth in schools and the inequities that are all too common therein, I approach this scholarly endeavor with an aim to shed light not solely on the status quo of U.S. schooling in the 21st century, but also the possibilities for change, innovation, and the promotion of social justice and equity for all members of the school community, especially those who have been historically marginalized.

Having joined Katie on this research journey, I interpet my participation as undergirded by a value for calling attention and giving voice to those who are not often heard (but frequently written and spoken about) in education research: teachers. Given the highly politicized and polarizing context of the current accountability era and neoliberal policy trends sweeping across the U.S., the perspectives, reflections, and insights from those at the front lines (our teachers) are too often silenced in favor of student growth percentiles on standardized assessments, value added models that reduce the complexity of classroom phenomena to a series of numbers, and rigid curricular standards that further cements a narrow body of knowledge as the primary instructional focus in classrooms. My hope is that this work will shed light on the multiple challenges, experiences, tensions, and opportunities frequently encountered by novice educators serving students in most need of a quality education.

Although I myself did not have a relationship with the participants in this study, I have previously taught in professional contexts similar to those discussed in this text. Drawing from that well of past professional practice, my own sense of self of having been a non-mainstream student in the P-12 classes I attended P-12 (I was one of the few Hispanic students in my classes), and living as a gay man in a country where thus far only 19 states and the District of Columbia have passed laws preventing LGBT Americans from employment discrimination, equity issues and the affirmative inclusion of all members of the school community are not solely issues of academic or scholarly interest, but also deeply personal ones as well. Thus, my engagement with these cases is guided by this interest and connects to my own biography as an integral part of the researcher assemblage I bring to this endeavor.

TEACHING-ASSEMBLAGES

INTRODUCTION

In this chapter, we think with the concepts of *assemblage* and *becoming* in and through the case of Mauro, who taught ninth grade (freshman) environmental science and 11/12th grade (upperclassman) earth science at Lincoln High School. We chose to use *assemblage* for this case in particular because, in examining the ways that the multiplicities of Mauro's classes worked together, they produced very different teaching practices. Further, Mauro himself produced different teacher subjectivities— or *became-different*—in relation to his freshmen or upperclassmen classes.

According to Deleuze and Guattari (1987), assemblages consist of a horizontal axis with two parts: its content, or human and material elements (students, teacher, desks, physical space, and the ways these connect) and its expressions (language and other discursive elements produced by, and producing, the assemblage). On a vertical axis, the assemblage has both reterritorializing aspects that stabilize it and "cutting edges of deterritorialization, that carry it away" (p. 108). We begin with a brief discussion of Mauro himself and the general characteristics of the school setting (elements each set of classes shared)—which are part of the "content" of the horizontal axis of the assemblages. We then move into discussions of each assemblage's different components-its content and expressions – and discuss how they worked together to produce particular patterns of instruction and Mauro's processes of becoming-teacher (the deterritorializing and reterritorializing functioning of the assemblages). However, because separating these elements enforces an artificial segmentation into component parts of an assemblage, we acknowledge that, rather than a map, a static representation of reality, or a tracing, is produced. To "plug the tracings back into the map" (Deleuze & Guattari, 1987, p. 13)—that is, to attempt to express the assemblages in their "thisness" or haeccity, their entangled complexity—we supplement this analysis with richly descriptive vignettes of moments of teaching practice.

Throughout the chapter, we suggest that the content and expression of Mauro's 12th/11th grade assemblages created a smoother space for deterritorialized edges— that is, it created conditions where Mauro could teach in ways that broke from the dominant methods of instruction to which urban students of color are normally subjected. In his ninth grade classes, however, the elements of the assemblage and their "collective assemblage of enunciation" (p. 108)—the discourses they produced and that produced them—made for a much more striated space where Mauro often reproduced a more authoritative social dynamic and teacher-led instructional patterns, and was "subjectivized" as a strict disciplinarian.

MAURO AND LINCOLN HIGH SCHOOL

Mauro was twenty-four, the child of Latino immigrants, and was the first person in his family to attend college. He grew up in a predominantly Spanish-speaking household and, despite remembering that he "was never read to as a child," attended one of the most prestigious Ivy League colleges in the US. In college, he developed a passion for environmental justice, and after finishing his degree, attended the NUTR because he was drawn to its social justice focus. When describing the teaching orientation he desired to enact in his first year of teaching, Mauro stressed that he valued critical thinking above all else. Rather than considering his job as a teacher of science content, he preferred to think of it as teaching "thinking processes in science." His residency year had been spent in a special education inclusion setting, and from this experience he had developed the belief that the best learning happens in one-on-one or small group settings.

Lincoln High School was a large school in one of the city's working class neighborhoods that served approximately 1250 students, the majority of whom were first generation Portuguese, Dominican, or Puerto Rican students, with smaller populations of Black students and students from other nations around the world. Nearly 20% of the students were classified as special needs, and approximately 15% were English learners, although many more than that spoke languages other than English at home. Mauro had a mentor, a relatively new physics teacher, and was part of a department where he shared a common planning period with other earth science teachers (although not with the other environmental science teachers). Both of Mauro's classes were "low track" classes—that is, they were made up of students who were not considered to have strong enough mathematic skills to be successful in the college-preparatory alternatives of physics (9th grade) or chemistry (11th grade).

11TH GRADE TEACHING ASSEMBLAGES

In Mauro's 11th grade classes, his older students, who were close to graduating, and different contextual conditions enabled Mauro to build relationships with his students and enact pedagogical practices that were closer to those promoted by his preservice preparation program—that is, practices more likely to incorporate student-centered inquiry and collaborative learning. The students themselves brought certain qualities that created a "smoother" space right away for Mauro to begin the year able to enact the type of instruction that was consistent with his professed beliefs and his learning from his preservice program—such as problem-posing with students, facilitating paired or small group instruction so students could collaboratively construct knowledge, and differentiating and scaffolding for individual student needs. Most importantly, Mauro perceived them as "more mature" because they were older and more focused on graduating high school. Because of that maturity, he felt these students took a more practical attitude toward school and their assignments. He also expressed that many of the upperclassmen were open to the kind of thinking and questioning that Mauro asked of them, responding positively to the activities he brought to the classroom:

> With my upperclassmen, I've tried more of theorizing, and what do you think, and what do you know, and working off of prior knowledge, and really building up that prior knowledge, and again, using those critical thinking skills where, OK, we've identified what we already know, and these are things, these are observations, maybe not made by you, but made by somebody, so how do those observations synthesize into what we know now, or what you think you know is true now? …And again, the upper classmen have been more receptive to it.

The conditions surrounding earth science also contributed to this smooth space. Earth science was not a tested subject, which meant that he had considerable flexibility in lesson planning and content sequencing. He commented, "I'm fortunate enough…[to have] the flexibility of me creating the curriculum…so I can afford to say yes, let's spend more time on [earth science], whereas in environmental I don't get as many luxuries." In addition, Mauro felt he was "more successful" in his earth science classes because of his knowledge and experience of earth science, which he had gained the year prior: "I know the [earth science] content more…because I taught the content last year." Yet another enabling condition was his upperclassmen class sizes, which tended to have fewer than twenty students. He explained,

> …when I look at the data and when I look at the grades, my smaller classes just have better grades…and who knows if that's necessarily a reflection of me or a reflection of them, or all of the above, but…I mean, you know, functionally class size does have a determining effect on how students are able to learn things, so…regardless of who is the one making that change, I mean, smaller numbers are jut easier to work with.

Each of these elements—the mature, easy-going students, the flexibility of planning and lack of testing, Mauro's comfort and experience with the content, and small class sizes—enabled Mauro and his 11/12th graders to work out satisfactory social norms. Together Mauro and his students created a class environment that Mauro called "casual and authentic." During class, students often chatted with each other while they completed their assignments, but Mauro did not mind, since, as he put it, "they will also do their work at the end of the day." The small size of his classes also allowed Mauro to get to know his students personally, enabling him to learn about what he called "human dynamics…how they work with people."

The smooth social functioning produced by the assemblage as a whole created conditions within which Mauro was able to use several strategies to get students to actively participate in an activity or to elicit particular responses from them. For example, he was deliberately transparent about his decision-making in the course, which he felt was important for modeling reasoning for students. For example, he explained his decisions, such as moving the date of a test up one day ("I didn't want you to have the review on Thursday and then take the test on Monday") or, another day, he explained to a student why he wanted him to wait to go to the restroom until he was done giving directions. He noted, "I guess it's really emphasizing 'because', and having them realize that when they make decisions, they should make the ones that best suit them, and know why it best suits them." By giving students access to his reasoning for classroom decisions, Mauro sent the message that they were partners in the educational process.

Another negotiation strategy Mauro used was what he termed "side conversations." He described these as "[taking] the opportunity to get to know each other and then get back to work." Sometimes these side conversations took the form of discussions that began as students made connections from class content to their own topical wonderings, such as a conversation about religion and science that arose from a lesson about the Big Bang Theory. Other times, students were inspired to share personal stories sparked by a particular topic. For example, when introducing a scenario on density that included driving a car, one of Mauro's students excitedly told the class that he had just obtained his driver's license. The student briefly summarized his experience and his success with the driving test. Mauro congratulated the student, who beamed with pride, before refocusing the class: "So back to our scenario..."

From the conflux of enabling conditions, smooth social functioning, and positive interactions stemming from being transparent and having side conversations, Mauro's upperclassmen were more open to participating in lessons characterized by problem-posing, critical thinking, and small group exercises. In other words, Mauro was able to enact instruction both relatively consistent with his own stated pedagogical beliefs and those promoted by his initial teacher preparation program. For example, Mauro did indeed make questioning a cornerstone of his teaching in this set of classes, usually structuring his lessons around open-ended inquiries that asked students to consider the "how" or "why" of phenomena they were studying. As an illustration, to begin his unit on continental drift, Mauro asked students to begin by examining a map of the continents and considering the question: "How do you think the continents get their shape?" Later in the same lesson, the class watched a video that presented information about Wegner's theory of continental drift, which at first was not accepted by the science community. "So the focus is on *why*," Mauro told his class. "[Wegner] saw something and it made sense, but he wasn't explaining why...and in the science world, you need a 'why'." As they moved further into this unit, Mauro posed the following problem to students during another lesson: "The process of forming coal requires extremely hot temperatures. So, given what you already know about Pangaea and continental drift, why might there be coal in New Jersey? And how might that provide evidence to support the theory of continental drift?"

In other lessons, Mauro provided hands-on, physical demonstrations or experiential activities that asked students to practice scientific skills, such as observing, hypothesizing, and theorizing about a possible outcome. In a class lesson on density, for instance, students partnered up to analyze the following scenario: Two people were off-roading, driving through mud, and abruptly crossed over to a cement surface. Mauro asked students to predict, given what they had learned about density, what might happen to the car when it moved from the mud to the cement. Once students had grappled with the problem together, Mauro asked for two volunteers to come to the middle of the room and demonstrate the idea. "Each of you are a front wheel," he told them, handing them a meter stick to hold between them that would serve as the car's axle. Mauro then asked other students in the class to call out their predictions about what would happen when the vehicle crossed over from the mud to the cement, and the student volunteers, as the car, performed the other students' guesses.

Because students tended to work together productively, in his 11/12th grade classes Mauro often used paired or small group instruction to differentiate learning. Mauro often included in his lessons individual, paired, or small group activities in which students supported each other during assignments while he circulated the room. During this time he checked in with students individually or as a small group, asking probing questions and working with those who needed more or different scaffolding. He thought this kind of activity allowed students to "go at their own pace...create their own story." Some of the collaborative activities were short theorizing breaks within a larger activity, such as a task where Mauro provided a graphic of underwater volcanic activity and asked students to hypothesize in pairs about what happened to the rocks that were produced underneath the ocean over time. Others spanned longer periods, such as a review activity that provided a set of essential questions for the unit. Mauro asked students to work in small groups for the entire period, while he checked in with each group and concentrated his time working more intensively with students who needed additional help or had been absent during the unit.

Mauro also constructed a situated subjectivity—what Deleuze and Guattari call an "individuation," or a momentary actualization of a subject—in relation to these classes and the ways these assemblages worked together. Because of the smoother social functioning of the classes and his own perceptions of success in teaching, Mauro described himself, as a teacher, being "much happier" and "natural, casual" in these classes. He felt like he could "be myself" and was likely to react to classroom situations in an easy-going manner, which helped maintain mostly fluid, smooth assemblage function. For example, during the unit on Continental drift, Mauro had an activity on a PowerPoint projected onto the whiteboard from his laptop. The next slide contained the answers, and when Mauro had his back turned, one student called out, "Hey! He cheated!" Mauro spun around to see a student had moved his powerpoint forward one slide. Rather than becoming angry for either handling his laptop or revealing the answers, Mauro just laughed and moved the slide back. Afterward, he reflected that, even had students copied the answer, he would have just asked them to explain how they got it. However, he also admitted that his reaction would have been very different had this event occurred in one of his ninth classes.

VISUALIZING CRYSTALLIZATION

Mauro was conducting a short demonstration to give students a visual of crystallization, using a test tube of salt, boiling water, and a bucket of ice water. After using familiar scenarios (making coffee, jello) to elicit that salt would dissolve in "supersaturated solution" (hot water), he then told them he was going to submerge the test tube with the dissolved salt solution in cold water, and asked them to predict what would happen.

Students offered several ideas: "It will explode!" "It will evaporate!" "It will turn hard!" Mauro placed the test tube in the water. "OK, let's see if it takes." As he waited, Mauro asked the class, "This is Epsom salt, has anyone ever worked with that?"

"Yeah," a student in the front said, "That's like, what you soak your feet in."

"What's the difference between Epsom salt and regular salt?" Another student asked.

"It's got bigger crystals," replied Mauro.

"And you can eat it!" said another student.

"Yeah," Mauro laughed as he pulled the test tube from the water, "It's good if you need to, uh, flush your body out."

"Gross!" groaned a student, as his meaning dawned on her.

Mauro walked around to each table, showing students that the solution was becoming cloudy and crystals of salt were starting to form. One girl exclaimed, "Whoa! It turned to ice! Oh, my god, Becky!" Mauro and several students around her laughed in reference to a line from an old hip-hop anthem.

"OK," Mauro said, returning to the front of the room. "So what did we end up seeing?"

Students yelled out their thoughts: "It's little balls of salt." "It's turning hard." "It's like a ball of ice."

Mauro retrieved a second test tube from his desk and held it up. "OK, so it was a liquid and now it's turning into a solid...over time it's going to look like this." He rotated between the tables so all the students could see that the test tube contained nothing but solid salt crystals.

After summarizing the process they had just witnessed, Mauro asked, "So what does this have to do with today? This is the same way that rocks form."

On the board, Mauro created the following chart.

Supersaturated solution=	*Ocean water*
Ice water=	*Rocks*
Salt Crystals=	*Lava with metals*

"So here you've got your story about the hot water solution, your ice water, and your crystals. I'm saying that this story" – *he gestured to the column on the*

right – *"is the same way that rocks form. So try to match up which of these"*— *pointing to the salt column*—*"matches up with these. So these are an analogy for these. Take thirty seconds in your notebook." As students worked, Mauro circulated between the tables, checking work over students' shoulders.*

"OK, who would like to pick one and match it up?"

"Ice water and ocean water," offered a student.

"OK, and why are you doing that?"

"Because they are both cold."

After eliciting answers for the other two, he summarized, "OK, so the story you could tell for the salt crystals, you could tell for the rocks here. So to give you a picture…" Mauro picked up a whiteboard marker and drew a picture of an underground volcano. "So here's our problem…lava keeps pushing up and rocks keep forming…so where are these rocks going? So take thirty seconds to get your thoughts down. So this lava keeps coming out and rocks are being made, so what is going to happen to the rocks over time? They have to go somewhere…where do they go? Write down what you think."

Some students began writing, but others either were still thinking about the problem, were having trouble coming up with something to write, or otherwise off-task (talking to their neighbor, playing with their cell phone or iPod, and so on). Mauro began to make his way around the room, stopping at two students who were chatting. Mauro squatted down and folded his arms atop their desk, resting his chin on his hands. "OK, gentlemen, what are you thinking?"

"It's building more rocks."

"Right, but where is it going to go?"

"The shore?"

Mauro turned and indicated the drawing on the board. "So here's our lava…this lava is going to keep pushing up more and more…there's so many rocks, it's like a crazy ice machine…what is going to happen to the rocks? Where will they go, where can they go?"

The student looked down at his paper. "I don't know, I don't know where they could go."

"Remember, this is deep in the ocean…where could it go?"

The student thought for a moment. "It would go above sea level?"

"So you are claiming they would rise?"

The student shook his head. "No, they would fall to the floor."

Mauro nodded toward the students' paper. "And then where would they go? Go ahead and get some thoughts down."

After a few more minutes of circulating, Mauro returned to the front of the room. "OK, let's bring it back…" Students were talking loudly by this point, and he had to repeat himself a few times. Mauro continued, "OK, a lot of you had interesting and well-thought out theories. Could anyone visually show what they think is going to happen on this map, on this picture?" He gestured to his drawing on the board. A girl got up, took the marker from him, and began to draw. "Does anyone else want

47

to come up and draw beside her?" Mauro asked, quickly grabbing another marker and sketching a duplicate volcano on the other side of the board. Another student rose and walked to the board to draw as well.

"Dani, can you explain your drawing to the class?" He asked. The girl had drawn rocks overflowing from the volcano and creating piles. She explained that the rocks would pile up and become mountains. "Interesting," said Mauro. "Emilio, can you explain yours?"

The second student had drawn the volcano similarly overflowing, with rocks creating piles and spreading out. "I was thinking more like islands...but the rocks are going to sink."

"And where do they keep going?" Asked Mauro.

"It's moving," said the student.

"What is IT?"

"It's the water...I don't know how to explain."

"It's OK," said Mauro, "You are right, and now we are going to watch a video on this, and it will tell you. We are going to watch a little of Bill Nye, the science guy!" A student in the back sang loudly, "BILL NYE THE SCIENCE GUY!" Mauro picked up the eraser and said," I apologize, but I have to erase this"—indicating the student drawings—"because I need it to project the video."

This vignette illustrates the willingness of the students to engage in questioning and theorizing and easy, harmonious social interactions, which seemed to help Mauro to pursue the objective of building students understanding of rock formation and seafloor spreading through active meaning-making processes. Like many of Mauro's 11/12th grade lessons, this class was planned around students engaging in questioning, observing, predicting, and theorizing processes. At each step a new connection was made: first students observed, predicted, and theorized about the salt crystal demonstration; then made a connection from that "story" to one about rocks forming in our oceans. After adding a new bit of information about the continual creation of rocks under the sea, students again theorized, this time puzzling out where rocks went as they were created. These theories were shared, and new information linking the students' thoughts to a video on seafloor spreading was provided. At each step, Mauro was dependent on student cooperation and responses to move forward. Because the students responded positively, choosing to engage in the activities, volunteer their thoughts, and participate in a way Mauro thought was appropriate, in return Mauro was much more "relaxed" in the way he interacted with them. He joked about "flushing out" one's body with Epsom salt, laughed along with students when a girl had a funny reaction to seeing the salt crystallizing before her eyes, and responded patiently when students took a few moments to get back to the task at hand or did not immediately start on the activity that had been assigned. All these elements contributed to the relative "smoothness" of the lesson on the particular day, and ultimately contributed to Mauro's ability to teach in ways that broke from the status quo of lecture-based instruction and instructional norms in urban schools.

9TH GRADE TEACHING ASSEMBLAGES

Mauro's ninth grade assemblages presented considerably more constraining elements than his eleventh grade assemblages. His ninth grade classes were both large, topping thirty students each. He also had them in two different classrooms, one after the other: his second period environmental science class was directly after another teacher's physics class, leaving him only minutes to set up between classes. He then taught eleventh grade back in his main classroom, and while the eleventh graders went to lunch after third period, he had another environmental class coming in, for which he again had little time to prepare. Environmental science was also a tested subject within the district, which meant that Mauro was responsible for teaching the students a particular set of skills and understandings on which they would be assessed via two district-wide exams (and to which his own teaching evaluation would be tied). Because the subject was tested at the end of each semester, environmental science teachers were also required to follow a particular curriculum sequence. While they provided a pacing guide, Mauro found it relatively useless because it did not account for the various holidays and school scheduling constraints. This also meant that he felt pressed for time in covering the material on which students would be tested. He explained,

> …They don't consider a lot of the scheduling and testing, and they don't even factor in finals half the time…they even include June, and we don't even teach in June, because the finals happen a week before school ends, so you've lost a week there, and you lose weeks in November, because November is a very unproductive, dysfunctional month, and they don't account for that. They just see the school year as being 186 days…and they said, OK, that's 92 classes, this is how this goes…so in Environmental we are rushing a lot more.

Mauro himself felt less prepared both with teaching the environmental science content and working with ninth grade students more generally. Although his mentor had taught environmental science, Mauro's responsibilities during the previous year had mostly centered on the eleventh grade earth science class, and he had not had much opportunity to teach the content or interact with ninth grade students in a teaching capacity. Additionally, his responsibilities in leading the earth science common planning meetings, and having a different preparatory period than the other environmental science teachers, complicated his ability to collaborate with other teachers in his discipline and limited the time he had to dedicate to environmental science planning. Mauro commented, "I have to focus so much on Earth [science] that I depend on other people to invest in the environmental, and I'm not there for common planning—Earth is my prep."

The students themselves also contributed elements that Mauro considered to be constraining factors in his ability to "teach differently." These included being "overwhelmed" with the transition to high school, a resistance to inquiry and critical thinking, a less friendly social dynamic, and what Mauro perceived as less-developed self-regulatory skills. Because they were coming from eighth grade, Mauro thought that his students were challenged by the transition to high school, where there was a sudden shift in the independent learning and behavior expected of them.

> I think [they are] just overwhelmed with life, too, is what it really comes down to... The expectations have skyrocketed between you know, middle school and high school, and whatever those expectations might look like, there's just more of them, and I think that's what's confusing to them.

His ninth graders were also not as open as his upper classmen to inquiry-based lessons, and Mauro believed that beginning the year with lessons requiring students to engage in inquiry-based activities had produced immediate resistance. Mauro explained, "[I] threw in all of my inquiry cards at once with my freshmen and I think it really overwhelmed them." His inquiry-based activities, which often asked students to critically analyze information and construct understanding about environmental science topics such as evolution and symbiotic relationships, required a level of active learning and deep thinking that Mauro believed the ninth graders had not been exposed to in middle school. In turn, students were often uncooperative during these types of activities. Mauro felt that the ninth graders' previous experiences with a more traditional, transmission type of learning had conditioned them to expect passive learning experiences where they were simply given information to memorize: "I think...it's that whole spoonfed mentality, where they don't know how to cope with somebody letting them think about anything, where they just want the answers." The ninth graders' resistance created disequilibrium for Mauro, whose beliefs about teaching were so firmly grounded in the criticality of thinking processes. He reflected,

> I'm really shocked by how little thinking they want to do, and like, how uncomfortable it is for me to be in an environment that functions around non-thinking... I don't think they know why it's important to think, which is a really odd realization.

While Mauro often commented on the "organic" and amiable collective demeanor of his upperclassmen, which contributed to the smoothness of collaborative work, his freshmen were more unpredictable in their peer interactions. His ninth grade students were more likely to engage in teasing, bullying, or antagonizing behavior, and classes were sometimes interrupted as students made insulting remarks to each other. During a class on biodiversity, one male student called out across the room to a girl, "Hey, Keisha, your name is in my mouth!" The girl screamed back, "What the fuck you say?!" A shouting match broke out, and Mauro stopped the class to discuss appropriate language and behavior. He told the class, "Why do we need to talk about each other? Let's just move beyond [this]. At the most basic, my goal is to help you; your goal is to learn. So let's stick to that priority."

Mauro also acknowledged that his students struggled with "personal responsibility", and identified a disconnect between the ninth graders' sense of self-awareness and classroom events, which further complicated the social functioning of the ninth grade classes. He commented,

> The freshmen will have this *major* gap between, 'this is what other people are doing wrong that affects me', 'this is what other people do right that affects me', and 'this I what I do right that affects me', but *not* 'this what I did wrong that affects me.' So that's been hard.

These challenges and patterns of interactions led to difficulties negotiating social classroom norms that were agreeable to both Mauro and his ninth graders. In particular, there seemed to be a gap between Mauro's expectations and what some of his students were willing to do. Mauro did not believe that he had overly harsh behavioral expectations for students, but he wanted them to abide by what he considered to be very basic social norms. Mauro commented,

> I've had many conversations about, 'It's really not OK to do this, this, and this, in a class. It's just not OK, and these are the reasons why. But even then, the reasons aren't good enough. Like, it's not appropriate to hit each other…I don't know how to communicate to them otherwise, that these are things that are really valuable skills to have, everything from just…you know, respecting when someone is talking to…um, I mean I think the big one is just respecting who is talking and respecting your peers.

Despite having multiple conversations with Mauro over the course of the first few months, the students made little progress toward meeting his behavioral expectations as a whole. The ninth grade lessons observed were often punctuated by moments where Mauro would stop the lesson and wait for students to stop talking, rebuke students for an unwanted behavior or inappropriate reaction, or remind students of appropriate social norms. Some of the students reacted to these "pauses" in the lesson by chiding their fellow classmates, while others became more resistant. Although Mauro felt that stopping and waiting was a rational, logical approach—especially because he always explained his expectations and the reasons for them clearly—the students did not agree. After one such class that was "shut down," Mauro related, "A few students were telling me, like, they think I put them down! And I was like, no! And I was…reinforming them that, my investment is to all of you, like 100%."

Mauro attempted to negotiate with his ninth grade students in similar ways to his 11/12th graders to achieve cooperation, but his efforts at "side conversations" and transparency produced very different responses in his ninth grade classes. The tangential in-class chats, which had been so successful in building relationships with his upperclassmen, largely failed with his ninth graders because he was not able to refocus them, and this meant that he was not able to get to know his freshman as well.

> If I even choose to sort of, engage them in whatever social conversation they are having about life, it can get carried away, and then I can't redirect them. So it comes to that, where, definitely my relationships with the freshman are not as strong as the upper classmen. They just in no way are. …[my upper classmen and I] take the opportunities to get to know each other and then we go back to doing work…the freshmen, it just can't be afforded to them.

His attempts to be transparent were also not as well received in his ninth grade classes. He shared, "The freshmen have just been so difficult, to give them an honest conversation, I, I don't think they fully get (pause) why I choose to be honest with them, or why adults should be honest with them, or (pause) I don't fully know." His attempts to discuss rationales behind classroom assignments of behavioral expectations were met with disbelief by students, who thought Mauro "was not … willing to listen, or to identify their needs with them." To promote honesty and candor with his students, Mauro tried asking for feedback from his students. He remarked, "I don't think a lot of the teachers are willing to hear the needs and demands of the students, and I think that's where I really want to stamp my mark."

Although at first his ninth graders were hesitant to speak to him about instructional matters in class, they soon began to voice their discontent, especially regarding inquiry. "They've started to push back, and I've been willing to let them push back, you know, imposing less inquiry with the freshmen, and I think their response is better" (he also mentioned here that this was in conjunction with the request of his department head to "cut down" on the inquiry). One student in particular, he explained, "flat out told me I was going too fast." To meet the expressed needs, he simplified his lessons. Although he thought his students responded more positively to his lessons, he worried about the overall rigor of the content.

> I think what's getting better is that I am simplifying a lot of things, and I think that's my biggest fear, is that I don't know how much of the rigor I am compromising…like today was the first lesson I've ever truly paced appropriately [with the ninth graders] but that's also because I cut out a lot of things I would have probably initially intended…I think that I fear, how much I am I lowering my expectations because I'm not fully aware yet of how to scaffold them to a point where I need them to be?

The elements of these teaching assemblages contributed to an unpredictable social dynamic that created constant struggle between Mauro and his students and made it difficult to enact the kind of open-ended, fluid practice that characterized Mauro's earth science classes. Instead, to minimize opportunities for conflict, Mauro adopted a strategy of filling the class to the brim with structured activity. He shared,

With the freshmen, it really has to be, all eighty minutes are *booked*, and this is what we are doing at minute twenty, and this is what we are doing at minute thirty. Everything has to be scheduled because they—they still haven't developed that skill, that self-awareness, of 'when can I choose to do something' and 'when can I not do something.'

In general, Mauro's teaching of his ninth grade classes tended to be teacher-led and tightly structured in response to the unpredictability. For example, in one particular lesson during his evolution unit, Mauro focused on teaching five different types of relationships between organisms, using "emoticons" as an entry point into student learning. To begin, Mauro handed out a graphic organizer with a three-column chart providing space for students to record each type of relationship (first column), and define the term (second column). The third column consisted of two "emoticons" (a smiley face, straight face, or sad face) which students could use to denote the nature of the relationship between the organisms (symbolized by the emoticons). A symbiotic relationship, for example, would require students to draw two happy faces, since the relationship benefitted both organisms. Mauro led the class through the first two parts of the activity, using a powerpoint to provide the terms and definitions, stopped after the introduction of each term to ask students which emoticon they would assign to each animal in the relationship. After completing this organizer, Mauro guided students through a set of video clips that demonstrated the different types of organism relationships, asking students to determine the type and record it on a second organizer. The last part of the activity asked students to independently read scenarios and identify the relationships as described in each. As this example shows, the structure of this lesson was fairly traditional, with the teacher first providing information about organism relationships, then guiding students in applying the definitions, and finally having students practice using the information on their own. At the same time, however, this particular lesson also incorporated various media, as well as emoticons, an element of popular culture familiar to the students, which became a tool for meaning-making.

Because the behavior of his freshmen was unpredictable, at times Mauro also had to modify his lessons in the middle of a class session if the students were not responding or participating as he had planned. As one example, Mauro had planned a lesson that required students to work in groups to determine, given a particular set of circumstances, how an organism was likely to develop and evolve over time. However, in the time period leading up to this activity, his students were so rowdy that Mauro had to stop and refocus them multiple times on their current task. Finally, Mauro became so frustrated with his students and their lack of cooperation that he modified his plans on the spot, altering the part of the lesson that was intended to be interactive to one where he posed questions to the whole class and students individually answered the questions.

The unpredictable dysfunction of his ninth grade assemblages also contributed to Mauro's becoming more authoritarian and controlling in these settings. Mauro remarked, "there are some characteristics that are very 'un-me' with the first years, where there is this unnatural strictness that sometimes appears." He adopted this "persona" to be "effective" with his ninth graders, as they did not respond to his natural demeanor. "I become 'angstier' with those classes, because things are already dysfunctional...I feel like I have to be more serious and reactive with them." He found that this "performance" exhausted him and conflicted with his ideas about what student-teacher interactions should look like, but he was at a loss for other alternatives.

> I can tell [my ninth grade teaching] is a performance, because just how exhausted I am after those lessons, compared to lessons where I am...genuinely myself. Whereas in the lessons where I have to put on this, you know, bizarre façade to be effective, it's just, I'm still trying to figure out how I can put myself in those lessons and while still being effective.

Becoming a teacher who used more traditional methods of dominance to assert control over students caused internal conflict for Mauro and produced affective responses from him. He related,

> I had like, a brief spat where I just silenced the classroom. After school, [a student] was like, 'are you sad?' And then later, another student is like, 'are you mad?' and I'm just like, I have so many stages of grief right now, like I don't even know if my body could contain them all.

Mauro was uncomfortable with being subjectivized in this manner, and he was unsure whether he was "allowed" to express feelings in connection with his teaching, which created even more disequilibrium for him. Reflecting on this dilemma, he explained to me, "I think, for the first time, I actually felt (pause) disappointed anger. ...the frustration was so built up that it just, morphed into anger." He then stopped and wondered aloud, "The one thing is like, are we allowed to do that? That's what we are struggling with."

WAITING

It was 9:49 on a Tuesday morning. In Mauro's classroom, the ninth grade students were grouped at rectangular tables, sitting four and five to a table. Chatter filled the air as students passed a large, clear plastic tub filled with brightly wrapped candies of different varieties. Mauro had given directions for each student to take two pieces of candy while they worked on the "do-now," which asked students to identify the characteristics of a chameleon that they think might help him hunt for food. When the bucket made its way back to the front of the room, Mauro looked at it, and stopped the class, saying, "Hold on, I would like to make an announcement." When students continued to talk, he reached over and turned off the power on the smartboard. "OK, I'm waiting...." He glanced over at the table of students to his left, still talking. "Ladies, I need to make an announcement." They turned toward him and stopped talking, but another burst of laughter emanated from a table on the other side of the room. "I'm still waiting," Mauro said. Finally, he told the class why he had stopped: "The candy was supposed to be for part of the lesson. There were more than 80 pieces in this bucket, and if each of you took two, there would still be over half of the candy left." He held up the bucket so everyone could see that there were only a few pieces left at the bottom. "This was meant to be for teaching today, but now you have destroyed this teaching moment. Many of you took more than two. I'm not asking who did it, because I can't take it back now. But I just want to put it out there that by taking more candy than you were supposed to, now our lesson is going to be affected."

"You should know better than to trust us," a student said.

"I want to trust you. OK, let's move on." With that, Mauro refocused on the "do-now," soliciting students to share their thoughts. "OK, I'd like to get people's thoughts...what helps the chameleon to hunt?" Several students raised their hands, but others continued to talk with their table-mates. Mauro began to circulate the room, talking with students at individual tables and asking them to give their attention to the task at hand. After a few minutes of discussion, led by Mauro, about the camouflage and turret eyes of the chameleon, the volume in the room rose as students began talking again. Mauro stilled at the front of the room, crossing his arms over his chest. As students saw that he had paused, some called out, "Shhhhh!" Mauro told the class at large, "I'm waiting." As students continued to talk, he repeated himself a few times: "I'm still waiting...still waiting."

One student huffed, "The silent treatment. I hate the silent treatment!" Another student from the back commented, "I think maybe if you just told us to be quiet, maybe we would." Mauro did not reply to these comments, but continued to wait. "OK, can we move on now? I want to see what's next," yelled out a student. Mauro paused for another moment more, and then clicked through to the next slide, which provided information about the long tongue of the chameleon, which was used to catch prey.

As the lesson progressed, several times Mauro stopped the lesson to wait and gather the attention of the students. Sometimes he would request, "Let's hold off on the conversations," before announcing, "I'm waiting." With each subsequent pause, some of the students became more and more aggravated, and the pauses became longer as students continued to disregard Mauro's waiting strategy. About twenty minutes before the end of class, Mauro once again paused and told the class, "I said this before, I'm not going to start until it is quiet."

The student, Michelle, who had made several caustic remarks about the "silent treatment," burst out, "The silent treatment is mad immature, yo."

Mauro replied, "It beats yelling at all of you. It-"

Michelle interrupted, "It's so immature."

Other students began to talk, some agreeing with her. "Can I finish?" Mauro asked. "Just let me finish my thought, and then we can hear from other people. I've told you that I don't want to yell, and at this point, if I did, I would lose my voice."

Michelle shot back, "If you wanted a job where kids will be quiet when you give them the silent treatment, you should have taken a kindergarten job. This is high school. If you don't tell us to be quiet, tell us to shut up, we aren't going to listen. You are the teacher last time I checked. If you don't act a little tougher people aren't going to listen to you."

"It's not my business to tell you to shut up or be quiet. I want you to develop some self-awareness around when it's OK to talk and when it's not. If you can develop those skills, then we could have discussions, rather than me standing up here talking all the time," Mauro responded.

Michelle said, "Well you can continue on with your silent treatment if you think you are actually getting somewhere. Who else thinks it doesn't work?" A smattering of hands rose. "I've got four, five, six people that agree with me. Even the new kid. First time in this class and he agrees with me."

Mauro crossed his hands over his chest. "All right, well you can think that if you want." He stood silently, gazing at the class.

Michelle burst out, "So you are going to still wait it out? You're not going to do something about it? What kind of teacher does that?"

Mauro said calmly, "Michelle, why don't you stay after class for me."

"I gotta go to gym."

"I'll write you a pass."

"Fine. Whatever."

"I just want to help you all answer these questions…let's leave it at that."

Mauro picked up with the activity, continuing to discuss adaptation for the last few minutes of class. After the bell rang, Mauro called out for Michelle to stay behind and talk to him.

Michelle told him, "You have to be tough on us. The students see you as soft and weak. We talk before this class, we talk after this class, and we say how easy it is, and it's basically a free period. You need to step up, and maybe we can get our stuff done." Mauro explained, "It's not that I'm soft. I just don't think it's right for me to tell you to shut up. I choose this method because I want to help you learn to self-regulate."

This vignette shows how the unpredictable and resistant responses of students and various mismatches between student and teacher expectations contributed to overall dysfunction. In the beginning of the lesson, Mauro had passed out a multi-variety tub of candy, asking students to take two pieces each. His plan was to use the leftover candy as an evolutionary analogy to discuss how species adapted to survive over time. However, the students instead took several pieces of candy each, not leaving enough candy for Mauro to make the analogy, and prompting him to tell the class they had "destroyed" his "teachable moment." Students again responded in a way that evidenced a disconnect between Mauro and his students: one student told him, "You should know better than to trust us." This bewildered Mauro, who wanted to be able to build trust with his students not only for relationship purposes, but also because it would allow him to enact more experiential and open-ended practices.

Because students were talking to each other and not participating in the activity as Mauro desired, he adopted a strategy of "waiting," pausing the lesson until students acted in a way that he felt was appropriate (being quiet while someone else was speaking). His reasoning for this move, which he had communicated to students many times, was because he thought it was wrong and disrespectful for him to tell students to "shut up," and he wanted students to learn to regulate their own behavior, to recognize when it was appropriate to talk and when it was not. Although some students cooperated with this strategy, even "shushing" other students, others responded with indifference, continuing to talk with neighbors. Still others became contentious, expressing their distaste for "the silent treatment." One student, Michelle, thought this tactic was "immature," and several others voiced their preference for a more direct method, "Just tell us to be quiet!" This created an interesting conflict: while Mauro was choosing to use the strategy of "waiting" because he felt that it was more respectful than directly telling students to stop talking, many of the students disagreed. Mauro contributed his students' reaction to their conditioning, having spent so many years in more "traditional" classrooms with authoritarian teachers. This might have been the case, or this might have partially explained the student response. However, as Michelle's words to Mauro after the class indicate, the students might have also been asking for Mauro to be a "warm demander," to demonstrate caring with "firm, fair discipline, high standards and expectations, and an unwillingness to 'let students slide by'" (Irvine, 2003, p. 46).

SUMMARY

Mauro's case points to the complexity of transitioning to teaching and negotiating the conflux of elements present in the setting. His teaching of earth and environmental science classes diverged significantly due to differences in the confluence of factors at play between the two instructional settings, which affected his ability to engage students in planned instruction. This influenced what he was able to do with his preservice learning, as well as shaped his burgeoning teacher-selves. We argue that viewing Mauro's teaching as assemblage—an amalgam of teacher-students-classroom-school and broader policy context elements—offers a way to discuss the practices of a first-year teacher, or any other type of teacher for that matter, as constructed by a multitude of influences. Considering Mauro's two sets of classes as their own teaching-assemblages allows for a more complex discussion of teaching, one that avoids depicting instruction as a set of actions that are either fully controlled by the teacher or fully determined by factors beyond the teacher's control. This perspective generates a more nuanced understanding of the production of Mauro's divergent practices, negotiations, and constructions of teacher-self.

Although each assemblage had some elements in common—such as Mauro himself, the school setting, and a common student demographic—these "plugged into" or came into composition with each assemblage differently. In the earth science classes, freedom from testing, familiarity with the content, and relatively small classes worked well with the maturity of the upperclassmen to provide conditions that enabled Mauro to build relationships with his upperclassmen that facilitated their negotiation of student-centered instructional practices he brought to teaching from his preservice program. The productive interactions between Mauro and his students, as well as Mauro's feelings of success in his teaching, fed into his construction of a positive teacher identity that "individuated," or temporally materialized, in relation to these classes. In contrast, Mauro was not able to build the same productive relationships and level of student cooperation with his ninth graders. The combination of contextual factors (testing, Mauro's lack of familiarity with the curriculum, and larger class sizes) and student responses created a classroom environment with student opposition and tense teacher-student interactions. Not only did Mauro's teaching become more rigid and teacher-led in environmental science, but he also began to develop a teacher identity in these classes as a "strict teacher."

MOLAR AND MOLECULAR ACTIVITY

INTRODUCTION

In this chapter, we discuss Deleuze and Guattari's (1987) concepts of molar lines, molecular lines, and lines of flight, by examining the case study of Bruce, a first year physics teacher. A graduate of one of the most highly prestigious and well-known Jewish universities in the United States, Bruce possessed degrees in physics, theater arts, and Jewish studies. Although this 25-year-old native of the Northeastern United States initially sought to complete a PhD and become a professor of science, after one semester of study he rethought his career path and elected to pursue a career in teaching. Soon thereafter he came across an advertisement for the NUTR and, given its social justice and equity focus, applied to the program. Bruce commenced his first year of teaching with a desire to serve as a quality teacher for urban and underprivileged students. His story reflects how, despite his desire to construct a classroom environment centered on principles of social justice and equity minded pedagogy, interacting internal and external challenges mitigated his capacity to do so. Thus, Bruce was unable to wholly "transfer" the pedagogy he learned during his time in the NUTR into his first-year teaching practices. Instead, he needed to identify ways of negotiating his pedagogy, his relationships with students, and his relationships with colleagues and educational leaders to persevere in his professional role as teacher and to align the professional identity he desired to enact with the ones which unfolded and transpired in his classroom.

Deleuze and Guattari (1987) conceive of *molar lines* as those forces, elements, conditions, or thoughts that serve to undergird the status quo, providing a reference point for reality as is, the possible, and the conceivable. Molar lines are taken as the "given" of any situation, encompassing the tacit assumptions, expectations, and understandings that inform and contribute to the routine operationalization or undertaking of an activity, function, or interaction. Examples of molar lines in education include the striated schedule of the school day, federal, state and local school policies, academic standards and curriculum, and the hierarchal relationship between teachers and school administrators.

Molar lines such as these are enacted and supported through the individual and collective actions and perspectives of individuals and groups, or *molecular lines*. Deleuze and Guattari (1987) suggest that molecular lines serve to carry out and perpetuate the molar lines in society. The daily tasks, activities, and engagements among members of the school community at large contribute to the upholding of the above referenced molar lines. Teachers instruct in accord with academic standards and curricula adopted by their districts and approved of by the state. Students are expected to demonstrate their internalization of the information and skills taught to them on standardized academic assessments and tests. School leaders influence the careers and livelihoods of teachers by making decisions regarding their evaluations and the granting of tenure. Each of these is an example of molecular activity in schools.

Yet breaks from the status quo or norms do occur via *lines of flight*. Lines of flight can emerge organically, reconstructing what had previously been assumed to be fixed and offering the possibility of an alternative. Although not all lines of flight are sustained, Deleuze and Guattari (1987) suggest that they are absorbed or subsumed by the molar. Collectively, over time, these lines of flight contribute to the shuffling and rearrangement of the segments that make up the molar structures of society and its various institutions. Social change thus emerges through the collective over and throughout a temporal sequence.

Bruce's case highlights how internal constraints (including his "molar" conceptualizations of teaching and learning and the role of teachers) and external constraints (conditions and actors in the school) unfolded and shaped his capacity to enact the kind of teaching practices Bruce learned during his time in the NUTR. Throughout the chapter, we suggest that the confluence of elements that constrained and enabled Bruce's teaching reflects the non-linear progression and transfer of preservice teacher learning into the first year of teaching. Bruce's case illustrates this process, as well as the internal, pedagogical, and professional negotiations he needed to traverse during his first year of teaching. Identifying elements of his experience as molar, molecular, and lines of flight provide an account of the multiplicities of which first year teachers are part and shed light on the ways these function as assemblages in the construction of first-year teaching practices.

BRUCE AND THE NORTHEASTERN PREPARATORY MAGNET SCHOOL

Bruce began his first year teaching at the relatively new Northeastern Preparatory Magnet School (NPMS), which focused on preparing students for college. Situated in a graffiti-ridden section of the city known for its high crime rates and poverty, NPMS was surrounded by run-down housing projects and abandoned buildings. The school building housed two other schools (both charters). Assigned to teach ninth grade physics, Bruce shared his classroom with a French teacher who claimed ownership over the space. Eventually, Bruce took advice from a school mentor and advocated for himself, indicating that he should be able to decorate a wall with mathematics and physics posters. Despite these decorative and educational additions, the room was not outfitted for physics nor materials or structures for classes to conduct scientific laboratory activities, nor were any physics textbooks or science materials provided.

As with the other residents of the NUTR, Bruce studied socio-cultural learning theories, inquiry-based learning and democratic teaching methods. Yet, while his peers experienced some tension in the shift from transmission-oriented instructional methods to more learner-center, inquiry based learning, Bruce was particularly challenged, finding these non-traditional approaches to teaching and learning to run counter to his own long-held views and beliefs on schooling. Despite this conceptual difficulty, Bruce made sufficient progress and by the conclusion of his second semester in the NUTR, the instructors and his mentor considered him ready to graduate. By the end of the program, he described his teaching style as "teacher-directed" but also stressed that he also believed that hands-on activities were integral to support students' engagement with physics concepts. He envisioned his classroom as filled with student-to-student dialogue and wanted to foster as much student autonomy as possible.

While his experiences in the NUTR supported a value for student-led inquiry learning, Bruce's professed views regarding his teaching style highlight how deeply-held beliefs and traditional cultural models can affect teachers' conceptions of what it means to be a teacher, as well as the ways these beliefs can persist through teacher preparation programs. Both of these points reflect molar lines of experience that followed him into his first year of teaching. At the onset of the academic year at NPMS, Bruce confessed that he "didn't want to shake the boat" with lessons that were "too out there" from what he thought other physics teachers were doing—hinting at the deeply ingrained molar lines (the long held beliefs and cultural scripts on teaching) that would contribute to his negotiation of teaching practice in the months to come. In addition to these internal challenges, Bruce was also confronted with multiple external challenges, such as a lack of resources and instructional materials and workplace dysfunction. In the following sections we describe the internal and external conflicts Bruce experienced, and how these enabled or hindered his ability to enact inquiry-based practices in his classroom.

BRUCE'S MOLAR LINES

As previously noted, Bruce began the school year with a strong desire to "play it safe". Given that all students in the school were required to take physics, many of them entered his classroom without a strong foundation on the requisite background knowledge and math skills necessary to engage with physics. Despite his professed belief in and desire for inquiry-based learning, Bruce's first several observed lessons were predominantly teacher-led, and many were aimed at providing the mathematical content that undergirded the physics concepts he sought to teach. Focused on isolated mathematical procedures, students participated in rote learning exercises that were often presented as unconnected to the complex physics topics that were central to the course. In post-lesson debriefs, Bruce explained that he considered it necessary for students to be able to complete the rote mathematical exercises as to build a foundation for conceptual understanding, which reflects the assumption that development precedes learning (Vygotsky, 1978)—that is, a student must develop and master particular skills prior to engaging in others. Ultimately, this stance is consistent with normative, transmission-based views of physics instruction. While participation in the NUTR fostered an appreciation for and acknowledgement of the value for inquiry-based learning, Bruce's long standing beliefs (his internal molar lines) constrained his confidence in his own capacity to enact such a pedagogy, an act that would veer beyond the space of "play[ing] it safe." Combined with his traditional beliefs about pedagogy, Bruce also harbored a belief that, as a novice educator, he was being watched closely by his leadership, and he was worried that teaching in a more inquiry-driven manner might not "work," which would put him at risk in his new position (although, as noted below, the school director had expressed her support for inquiry-based teaching). Illustrating this line of thinking, Bruce commented, "I don't think I can go as 'out there' when planning stuff. I can't just go, 'Hey! This is inquiry-based, let me try it and see if it works!' It's GOT to work".

Bruce's fear of the consequences of veering away from traditional forms of teaching physics, despite his willingness to "experiment" with non-traditional instruction, was also exacerbated by a change in educational leadership at the school. The former school director had indicated her preference for teaching through inquiry, valuing the innovative and student-centered approach aligned with the kind of learning Bruce experienced in the NUTR. Working with an educational leader who valued such practice, Bruce was initially inclined to "test out" inquiry-based learning, opening himself and his classroom to the various pedagogical scenarios that were possible in such a context. Although he seemed to retain core beliefs about traditional learning and teaching, school leadership was a factor that served to mitigate his internal conflict and promote a pedagogy aligned with the vision of the NUTR.

The new principal who began working in the school in November seemed less inclined toward innovative practice than the former, as Bruce perceived it. After we observed a lesson in which Bruce led the class through solving problems related to kinetics, Bruce once again returned to his explanation of being "safe" with his pedagogy. He articulated, "I'm trying to stay in the safe zone until I get some actual feedback from [the new principal]." "Staying in the safe zone" meant teaching in more traditional ways, which Bruce thought "pleased the powers that be." Bruce's perception of the new director appeared to be a molar, or normalizing, influence, that shaped his becoming in the beginning of his school year, inhibiting him from going "out there," or pursuing lines of flight of *teaching-differently*.

The new principal's preference for traditional teaching also increased Bruce's worries about his teaching evaluations. While the former principal had cultivated a comfortable environment that allowed students freedom in classrooms and the larger school environment, the new principal made discipline and structure her primary reform effort. In particular, she initiated a zero-tolerance plan that imposed stiff penalties for inappropriate student behaviors such as cursing and required that teachers defer all disciplinary measures to her. Although Bruce agreed that some structures were needed to increase student accountability for maintaining an orderly environment, he disagreed with the principal's direct, no-excuses disciplinary approach. He parricularly disliked that she tended to emphasize blanket consequences over investigating into circumstances around disciplinary infractions. He explained:

[Principal] will just come in during my class and talk to them…. [She will say] 'I don't care what your grades are, I don't care about any of that. You will get the full consequences.'…I would have addressed, 'Why did this happen? How did this happen?' instead of jumping right into consequences.

These differing ideological perspectives not only on teaching, but also on attending to and promoting safe, equitable, and affirmative learning environments for students, further challenged Bruce in his own pedagogy, and under the new school leadership, his belief in the need to engage in traditional pedagogy in his classroom was reinforced.

Nonetheless, at times Bruce did still attempt to enact inquiry-based learning. While internal molar lines largely dictated the molecular activity that unfolded in the classroom, occasional opportunities surfaced where Bruce felt "more safe" to "experiment" and venture forth in a non-normative lesson. While Bruce considered these lessons to be instances of *teaching differently*, such lessons still retained kernels of traditional aspects and elements of teaching. The following vignette illustrates Bruce's attempt at promoting collaborative problem solving. In the lesson, elements of traditional and non-traditional pedagogical approaches surface with mixed results for Bruce and for his students, reflecting the complexity of teaching and learning itself, and the non-linear transfer of preservice learning during novice years of practice.

COLLABORATIVE PROBLEM SOLVING

"Let's get started," Bruce called over the din of student voices as he entered the classroom. He glanced toward the desks, which were situated in a "U" shape, where students were talking to each other. Skirting the edge of the U and narrowly avoiding colliding with a student dancing by himself, Bruce made his way to the board and began to erase. He continued, "If I can have everyone's attention…" A few students turned and faced the board, while others continued to socialize. Bruce raised his voice. "YO! I have something for us to do now!" As the talking faded, his voice returned to normal volume. "You remember the homework? Of course you do! Did everybody do it?"

Several students called out at the same time. "I did it!" "I got my homework!"

Bruce picked up a piece of chalk and began to divide the board into three sections. "Of course you did! I need volunteers to do number 10, 11, and 12." Hands shot into the air, and Bruce handed out pieces of chalk to students to work on the dynamics problems. "Go for it…ok, do we have someone for number 12?" Each student approached the chalkboard and began copying their solutions. Meanwhile, Bruce asked two students who had been absent the day before to move to a side table to make up a quiz they had missed. After giving them each a quiz and getting them started, he began to pass back quizzes from earlier in the week. As he made his way around to each student, the teacher next door, Ms. Birch, entered the room. "Mr. Cohen, we need you to go get your picture taken."

Bruce looked up in surprise. "I'm in the middle of teaching!"

"It will only take a minute. I will cover for you," replied Ms. Birch.

Bruce nodded. "Keep working the problems," he said to his students as he left the classroom. The students at the board, one by one, finished their problems and each took a seat. With no assignment, students talked to one another, a few yelling across the room at other students.

After about five minutes, Bruce came back and thanked Ms. Birch for staying with his students. He quickly glanced at the board. "All right, did anyone get a different answer for number ten?" After reviewing the answers, he moved on to the next part of the lesson. "OK, is everyone ready to play the game? This game – we are going to up the stakes – this is actually worth extra credit points." He looked around at the students, who remained quiet. "What, you're not excited" I'm actually giving out extra credit points!"

As if on cue, students clapped, whistled, and some yelled "Yay!"

Bruce laughed. "OK, so I'm going to break you up into teams…"

"How many teams?" Asked a student.

"Last time we did six. So go ahead and separate the lab tables." Students obligingly began moving tables into groups. After they were settled, Bruce continued, "OK, so here are the rules of the game. I'm going to be giving you a paper with a variable on it. It's either going to be f, m, or a. You need to make a problem that other people will have a hard time solving. You can use kinematics equation one, two, or three to make this problem, or F=MA. And it's gotta be a word problem. I'm going to be putting the formulas on the board. Groups can be two or three people, but it can't be anyone who's taking a quiz currently."

Bruce retrieved a blue bucket from behind his desk. "All right, I'll go around, and let people pick their variable. The goal is to find the variable of your problem. You also have to be able to solve your own problem. So you will come up here –" he indicated the front of the room – "And read your problem. The rest of the class will have two minutes to solve it. If they can solve your question, they get a point. If you manage to stump the rest of the class, and still have a legitimate question, you get a point. So you want to make these problems as hard as possible, but still solvable. Get me?" He glanced around the room. "Everybody gets me? All right."

Bruce began rotating between groups, with students reaching in the bucket to choose a variable at random. Spotting a student sitting by himself, Bruce asked, "Where's your partner, David?"

David pointed to another group, where the other student had defected, dramatically announcing, "He betrayed me!"

Bruce called to the other student, "Come back here, you are with David." To the class at large, he announced, "OK, you have five minutes. I'm going to write the equations on the board."

As he wrote, several of the students called out questions, voicing their confusion over the assignment. "What are we supposed to be doing again?" Bruce stopped his writing to address the class and rephrase the directions. "I'm looking for a word problem."

A student put his head in his hands. "I'm confused," he muttered.

A student held up a worksheet from the previous week. "Can we use this?"

Bruce nodded. "You can use any resources you have available."

"Hey, Mr. C!" A student waved Bruce over. "Can you look at what we have?"

Bruce read the students' work and nods. "OK...so you've got three different people running at three different times. Tom runs for four seconds, Jerry runs for five seconds...how far does Tom go? Yeah, that's three pieces of data in there that have nothing to do with anything. That's a great idea."

He moved over to the next group, where three girls were loudly debating. "No it's not, that's the distance," one of the girls said. The other stood and leaned over her shoulder. "No- here's what I was thinking- you have the v_o and the x_o," she said, referring to the parts of the first and second kinematics equation.

"But if she's giving them 'a', it's a two step equation!"

"No, look! Think about it! It's gotta be three steps. They have to find 'v_o' first. Then they have to find 'a'. Then they have to plug that into that equation and—"

"But we have to give them time, though," a third group member interjected.

Another table called for Bruce to help. He moved over to their table, leaning down to talk to them. One held up his paper for inspection. "Mr. C, does this sound too easy?"

"Yes, it does," he said. "Just kidding, I haven't looked at it yet." He read the problem and pointed out, "75 pounds, that's a small truck." Continuing to read, he nodded his head. "I like it, I like it! So it falls under equation two and you are combining it with f=ma."

Cheers erupted from the table of girls. "Yeah! We got this!" One squealed, leaping from her chair in excitement.

After another few minutes, Bruce announced, "OK, two more minutes and then we'll solve some problems."

"Wait! Wait!" students protested.

Bruce pulled up a chair next to one of the students' tables. "All right, finish up, we're going to start calling on groups in a minute."

After a few more minutes, Bruce said, "OK, we are going to go counterclockwise, this way, starting with your group, because I know your question is ready."

"How come you can't start with Shanna's group?"

"NO!" The girls yelled in unison.

"Come on, said Bruce. "OK, you've got a minute and a half to solve this. If you have the answer, raise your hand. If you answer correctly in a minute and a half, you get an extra credit point. If no one does, and you can solve it for us, you get the extra credit point. Got it?"

Two students came to the front of the room. One read, "Aaliyah pushed a 70-foot—"

"I can't hear you!" "Louder!" said students in the audience.

The student raised his voice. "Aaliyah pushes a 70 kilogram rick down a cliff with an acceleration of 2.5 meters per second squared. What force does gravity pull a 70 kilogram rock with?"

"Wait...so Mr. Cohen, we have to find the acceleration? Because as far as I can see, it would be force divided by acceleration, just to get the mass."

Bruce shook his head. "You have to find the force, the force by which gravity pulls that rock with."

"But don't you have to find the acceleration?"

Bruce shook his head again, announcing, "30 seconds left!"

A student raised her hand. "686 newtons?"

"We have a winner! OK, 686 newtons, how is that?"

The student slid her hands across the desk. "Because you multiply 9.8, the gravity," she said, referring to the numerical value for the acceleration of gravity for a free-fall object.

"Aha! We didn't give you that it was 9.8. They got it!" Bruce said, standing and clapping. He glanced at the clock, seeing that class was nearly over. "OK- let's hurry! We've only got a few more minutes. Who's next?"

This vignette demonstrates several lines of flight that escape from the status quo of more traditional instruction. During the main activity, students were enthusiastically creating word problems, applying learning from both their kinetics and dynamics unit. Many of the students were engaged in rich student-to-student dialogue as they struggled together through an open-ended assignment that required both procedural and conceptual knowledge of physics concepts, as well as their own creativity. The roles the students and teacher played in the main part of the lesson also interrupted traditional teacher/student roles as provider and consumer of information, respectively. Bruce embraced a non-traditional teaching role in the collaborative problem-solving activity as a facilitator and expert other (Vygotsky, 1978), while students were active meaning-makers and co-constructors of knowledge.

Despite such progressive features, the lesson also highlights molar lines that worked to reinforce the status quo and contribute to tensions in Bruce's practice. The start of the class was complicated by a lack of organizing structure—the school bell operated on one of the other schools in the building, so the signal for class to begin was Bruce calling out, "Yo! I have something for us to do now!" The previous teacher in the room had left work on the board, which meant Bruce had to take time to erase it to make space for students to write. Aside from the homework problems, no warm-up that engaged the class as a whole was provided, which meant the majority of the class had no assignment for the first ten minutes of class. Two students were given a make-up test, which meant they were not able to take part in the activity. Bruce was also pulled out of class to get his picture taken, losing several more minutes of instructional time. Although he ventured to "test out" inquiry-based instruction, these molar lines inhibited Bruce's sense of self-efficacy in being able to enact such a practice. A closer analysis also illustrates contradictions between Bruce's stated beliefs and his practices. In his interviews, Bruce emphasized the collaborative and egalitarian nature of his classroom interactions, commenting:

> I've gotten in a habit of when the students are up at the board, I have them call on the other students. Instead of me...I want to give as much power to them as possible...so I let them call on the other students. "I have a question about your process." "Ok." just like that. And I stand back.

While Bruce did call students to share their homework answers in the beginning of class, no dialogue between students, peer review, or student questioning occurred. No explanations were elicited. While collaborative problem-solving and student-to-student talk occurred during the main part of the activity, when students shared afterward, the direction of talk was student-to-teacher only.

Another complicating factor was the ambiguity of the main assignment. Bruce gave verbal instructions, which several of the students found unclear or confusing. After giving initial instructions, Bruce had to spend several minutes reviewing the specifics of the exercise and answering questions about the activity. Although each of the groups of students seemed to grasp the objective and quickly became engaged in the assignment, the lost time due to lack of organization in the beginning of class, Bruce taking his picture, and having to repeat instructions meant that students were not able to finish their activity.

INSTITUTIONAL MOLAR LINES

The challenges and difficulties that Bruce experienced as he constructed his first-year pedagogy were not confined to internal elements. In conjunction with these, several external facets of the school environment coalesced as complicating forces for the kind of pedagogy that he wanted to more fully embrace. In this section, we explore these external constraints, or institutional molar lines, affecting Bruce's pedagogy. Specifically, we consider minimal resources and instructional support, lack of consistent induction and mentoring, and challenging student interactions as molar forces that informed the molecular enactment of Bruce's teaching.

As previously discussed, from the onset of the academic year, Bruce sought to enact the kind of pedagogy he was taught in his preservice teacher residency program. Despite this desire, he nonetheless worried about straying too far from the dominant notions of teaching and learning he believed his new principal supported. He also was concerned that if he were to fully implement practices such as learner-centered problem-solving, he would be unsuccessful in his teaching, and worried whether or not his students would "get" the content he sought to cover in class. This internal struggle was compounded by external constraints and conditions that increased his insecurity to employ a progressive pedagogy in his classes. Among these factors was a change in instructional leadership at the school, an administrative disruption that reinforced Bruce's internal struggle with progressive pedagogy. Thus, in conjunction with his internal struggle, the external condition of changing leadership (and Bruce's perception of the new principal as less inclined towards innovative practice) served to compound and inhibit the likelihood that Bruce would fully embrace this kind of teaching in his classes.

As previously discussed, Bruce became preoccupied with "playing it safe" and "remaining in the safe zone" when it came to his teaching. This preoccupation may have been somewhat informed by his own traditional beliefs about teaching and learning and compounded with his interactions with the new principal. The combination of these internal and external constraints coalesced and manifested with Bruce beginning to plan lessons and instruction based on his own ideas about how other PSI physics teachers in the district were teaching. Although he was not explicitly told to create his lessons based on such a summation, he somehow had developed the idea that he would be compared to other PSI teachers in his district and found lacking. During his final interview, Bruce expressed the following:

Bruce: I would like to do it the other way [in a more inquiry-based way], um, but I want to be sure that they can get this mechanical stuff. I am still being compared with the PSI [Progressive Science Initiative] teachers.

Katie: Who is comparing you?

Bruce: I'm assuming that, for observations and whatnot, I'm going to be compared to the PSI teachers.

Katie: Are there any other PSI teachers in this school?

Bruce: No.

Katie: So who's going to be comparing you? Your observations are going to be done by your principal, right?

Bruce: True, but if the principal goes to observe another physics course, and they are like, oh, it's completely math, and oh, Mr. Cohen is completely conceptual...I don't want to do something so out there from the other physics teachers in the district. Already I'm going out there.

Katie: So what I'm hearing is that you want your class and your teaching to also match the other physics teachers in the district?

Bruce: So that there's not a discontinuity...there's not a, 'Well, they are teaching this, why are you teaching something completely different?'

Fearing a negative evaluation (that could lead to employment termination), Bruce ultimately decided not to veer too far from a traditional physics teaching style or the curriculum approved and adopted by the school district. He therefore sought to "stick to the script", and for the most part follow lessons as outlined in the teacher manuals. Yet even compliance with this aspect of his professional context presented challenges that constrained his ability to even fully enact traditional teaching practices. For instance, there was a significant shortage of instructional materials and resources in Bruce's school. While most science classrooms in the school district had physical materials, resources and technology to support student learning, experimentation, and scientific inquiry, Bruce's classroom had no sinks, cabinets to store equipment, or lab tables. Bruce also identified the lack of laboratory or physics equipment for demonstrations of phenomena or to create experiments as a seriously limiting factor. Although he was under the impression when newly hired by the NPMS director that some materials and lab equipment would be ordered and supplied, this never occurred. Feeling constrained and unable to fully engage in lessons and activities to support student learning (and conduct the kinds of lessons he wanted to teach), he took initiative and eventually spoke to the school administration about the lack of resources. Bruce reported, "I was laughed at", and ultimately found it necessary to create materials of his own.

The few labs he was able to plan, he explained, were "invented out of stuff I already have [from home]...I have to actually build these labs from scratch." To provide his students with physics experiments and labs, he delved into his own collection of materials and objects, such as a set of Nerf guns, which he featured in two labs observed in this study. Creativity emerged as a central and requisite aspect of Bruce's teaching, and he found it necessary to employ whatever materials or resources were readily available in an innovative way to use in the classroom. During the course of the year he utilized chairs, a bowling ball, and towels for in-the-moment demonstrations of physics phenomena.

The dearth of physical resources made available by the school was also reflected in the lack of appropriate technological support and resources. Providing the rationale that the school was only temporarily housed in the building, the administration opted not to invest in updating the technological capabilities or information technology in the building. In conjunction with the formerly discussed internal constraints and challenging physical aspects of his professional environment, the lack of technology similarly affected Bruce's ability to enact lessons as he would have desired. In one instance, during a class where he intended to show a YouTube video to introduce Newton's three laws, the Internet was loading too slowly because of a poor connection. After fifteen minutes of trouble-shooting with lack of success, Bruce used his personal smart phone as a "WiFi Hotspot" in order to show the video. While he was eventually able to have students view the video, he nonetheless lost more than a third of his class period trying to find a way of doing so. Bruce elucidated, "You can know the technology and know it really well, like I do, but when push comes to shove and you don't have electricity in half your classroom, it becomes difficult to use that technology."

Unfortunately, Bruce was also negotiating these circumstances on his own without appropriate or consistent mentoring. He instead drew from his own long-term beliefs, insight gained from his preservice preparation, and in-the-moment decision making to persevere through a challenging context. Induction support was inconsistent (reflecting a common challenge among novice educators). Although he was assigned a school-based mentor, a veteran seventh grade science teacher, the teacher rarely came to observe and on occasions when he did, the visits were only a few minutes in length. The mentor, who Bruce characterized as very "traditional," was unable to provide support with inquiry-based activities and did little to ease or assist Bruce with the challenges he was facing.

Support in the form of a regular NUTR induction coach did not begin until the end of November, three months after the start of the school year. Bruce reflected, "I felt like I had been abandoned...I feel like I had been forgotten." A retired elementary school teacher, the induction coach was not knowledgeable about either physics content or social justice-focused pedagogy. Considering his mentor "not so useful", Bruce indicated that the coach was unable to provide feedback in these areas of instruction. Further, the coach frequently expressed that his time was limited and he had a multitude of administrative matters with which he needed to deal. For example, during one debrief regarding an inquiry-based lab, Bruce shared that he had asked the induction coach to observe his lessons and provide feedback, but "He said he had a long meeting at [university], and that was his five hours [for the week]." The lack of consistent and appropriate mentorship contributed to Bruce's feelings of inadequacy with inquiry-based activities. Both of these represented molar lines that supported more traditional practice.

MOLECULAR ACTIVITY WITH STUDENTS

The external conditions discussed above affected what Bruce was able to do in his classroom, his perspectives on teaching and learning, and ultimately the decisions he made on how best to work through the momentary and ongoing challenges in his professional context. Yet in spite of his sense of professional isolation, Bruce's professional enactment occurred in relation to his students. A central aspect in the molecular work of the classroom, or the day-to-day activity that occurred, were the relationships between Bruce and his students. Bruce interacted with students in a friendly and open manner, and students seemed to genuinely like him, potentially contributing to their enthusiasm toward the content. Despite occasional conflicts between students, relationships in the class appeared easygoing and casual, not only in interactions among students but between Bruce and the students themselves.

In one instance, for example, at the start of one lesson, a student was loudly rapping as Bruce checked homework. Bruce stopped in front of the student and listened for a moment, then asked, "Is that the best you got?" The student, in response, burst into a new verse about Bruce checking homework. Laughing, Bruce teased, "You need to work on your freestyling!" Likewise, during a class on free body diagrams, Bruce drew a stick figure of himself to supplement an illustration on the board. "Oooh, draw your beard!" called out one student. Bruce did so. Another student added, "Draw your hat!" Obligingly, Bruce drew a circle representing the yarmulke he always wore. "You gotta draw your stomach!" yelled a third student, holding his arms out in front of him to simulate a belly. "Hey!" Bruce scolded playfully, wagging his chalk as the room filled with laughter.

Developing this friendly rapport – an non-traditional element in historically dominant discourses of teachers – was thus a productive means of negotiating the numerous internal and external constraints. Establishing trust emerged as another central facet in the relationships Bruce sought to develop, which served to interrupt traditional power relations between teachers and students. One way of doing this was by giving out his home phone number and personal email at the beginning of the school year so students could contact him beyond the regular school hours. In his first interview, Bruce said, "I actually have had two students who have texted me so far. Which is cool! Um, it's a lot more personal, and um, actually showing that… you are not like, a robot." Fostering open lines of communication contributed to the molecular nature of Bruce's interactions with students, allowing for occasional lines of flight and managing occasions when respect and rapport was absent. For instance, a student cursed in class at Bruce after being informed that she was failing, and the principal suspended her for a week. In the debrief after the lesson, Bruce stated that he anticipated the need to let the student "cool down" for several days upon her return to school before approaching her to talk about the interaction. To his surprise, however, the student contacted him on her own before she ever set foot back in his classroom. Bruce described,

> I got an email from the student, apologizing and saying why it happened: "I had a rough day, I was having a bad social day, I was having a bad day with grades in general, you are the last [class of the day] and you were just there. It's not against you, I feel really bad and I apologize profusely." I mean, she didn't use the word profusely, but it was a very meaningful apology, with an explanation…She was like, "This is what was happening, I know it's no excuse, but I want to give you some background to let you know, this is how I feel about you. You just-you got me at a bad moment."

Over the course of the week, Bruce and the student continued to exchange emails and texts. By the time she came back to school he felt his relationship with her had changed and connected this event to a larger realization: "There's a lot more under the surface [with students]. As a whole, it reminded me that, yeah, intellectually I know there's a lot going on with the students, but this made it more real." This moment of honest communication between teacher and student in an out-of-school-setting, which also contributed to learning on the teacher's part, constitutes a line of flight, temporarily breaking each out of their static identities as teacher-student. When this line of flight was recaptured as the student returned to school and Bruce resumed his role, the shuffling of the molar lines that separate teacher and student was evident in the improved relationship between the two.

Bruce also was able to cultivate special relationships with certain students that were identified by the school as "trouble-makers" (a molar identity category). These relationships, and the interactions that followed, allowed the students to break from the norm of their identities and become-different. Two students in particular, Edmund and Joy, demonstrate this trend. During observations, Bruce frequently called on Edmund, a quiet, husky African-American student, to assist him with demonstrations of phenomena or help with classroom tasks, such as handing out materials for projects. Further, during an observed lab activity, Bruce deliberately gave Edmund a leadership role. After the group had shown Bruce their experiment plans and obtained his approval, he tossed Edmund a large automatic Nerf Gun, calling over his shoulder, "OK! Edmund's in charge!" Also in Bruce's study hall period, Bruce discussed a project where he and Edmund deconstructed and rebuilt a Wii. Whereas Edmund occupied the fixed, molar identity category of resistant student who was constantly in trouble in other classes, in Bruce's he was able to take on other identities, such as class leader, a successful physics student, deserving of positive teacher attention. Unfortunately, after the winter recess, Bruce related that the principal had sent Edmund back to his neighborhood school due to repeated behavior infractions in his other classes.

Like Edmund, Joy was a student who was assigned to the molar category of "trouble-making student" outside Bruce's classroom. In Bruce's class, however, Joy was the "star student," often the first to volunteer to solve a problem on the board or join Bruce in demonstrating physics phenomena. Bruce explained that he thought she responded so well to him because he "treat[ed] her like an adult, consistently." Her comfort in his classroom was particularly in evidence during a day when she was sent out of one of her other classes. Bruce shared,

> So she was kicked out of one of her other classes because she is not very respectful to her other teachers. So she was kicked out of another class, and she wanted to stay in my class and help out. I was like, ok, I have no complaints there, all right. 'Cause she already had the same lesson earlier in the day, and I had the same lesson with the other two classes. So she stayed and she was actually my teaching assistant. She would go around to tables, checking work, which is good because she actually has a very sharp understanding of the content.

Another element contributing to student enthusiasm and cooperation was Bruce's occasionally creative approaches to lessons. As previously noted, Bruce owned an extensive collection of Nerf guns of many different varieties, and he designed several activities using these with the students. The activities involving Nerf guns always drew excitement from the students, as they were a line of flight, a break from the norm – a toy, a "fun" implement that blurred the boundary between learning and play. Another example involved a series of videos Bruce created for his students during the September Jewish holidays. Knowing he would miss multiple days of school, Bruce created interactive, full-class-length videos for the substitute teacher to play for the students. These videos presented content using various pop culture materials. For instance, one video was created, as he described it, "in Cloverfield style" (the style of a particular horror film). As the video began, Bruce theatrically explained that the school had been attacked by zombies – he was trapped in the classroom, and the students had to save him by figuring out the trajectory he would need to fire his weapon and slay the zombies outside the door.

These smooth student-teacher interactions may have contributed to Bruce's continuing to consider and experiment with more active learning opportunities despite the multiple constraining circumstances and conditions. Although his classes were usually teacher-led, he did seek opportunities for collaborative student learning. As an example, the following vignette illustrates a lesson in Bruce's class where he sought to provide a hands on learning activity (drawn from his preservice learning) yet still adopting a teacher-led format (an attempt to not veer 'too far out' in his teaching). The instructional episode serves as a portrait of the ways Bruce negotiated student behavior through his teacher-student interactions, engaged in on the spot decision making to propel the lesson forward, and creatively utilized his personal resources (the Nerf collection) to compensate for a lack of instructional materials.

THE NERF DEMONSTRATION

The classroom echoed with a cacophony of excited teenage voices. Bruce walked into the classroom, signaling the start of class (the bells were synced to the elementary school, one of the three schools with which Northeastern College Prep was located). He crossed to the desk in the corner, where at least ten nerf guns of differing sizes and design were laid out neatly in two rows, their brightly colored plastic vermilion and chartreuse exteriors a beacon in the artificial light of the classroom. The pitch grew higher as the students spied Bruce, in his uniform of khaki pants, a short-sleeved button-down oxford, and a multi-colored yarmulke perched on top of his head. One student yelled to the rest of the class, "Shut up! It's Nerf time!"

"That's right," Bruce called out over the noise. He chose two Nerf guns and held one in each hand, pointing in different directions. Several students cheered loudly. "Right now," Bruce continued, "We are going to ponder a question not even Newton could figure out." He brandished the two weapons, showing students that the two Nerf guns he held were designed differently. "Which one shoots faster?"

The room filled with student voices, shouting their choice. "OK now—raise your hand—this one is mechanical"—he raised the gun in his right hand and about six students raised their hands—"and this one is automatic." The remainder of the hands in the class shot into the air. "OK, pass this over to Benjamin." He passed one of the guns to the student next to him, who dutifully, if regretfully, passed the gun to a tall, stocky African-American boy a few seats down. "Benjamin—take that and go towards the back." As Benjamin took the gun and positioned himself in the back of the room, Bruce turned to the student on his other side and said, "Now just so you know—these are soft. They don't hurt when you shoot them." He shot the student in the arm, and an orange foam dart bounced off the boy's arm. The class broke into laughter. Bruce continued, "But still, no shooting in the face. OK, now how are we going to test this?"

"Shoot! Shoot him!" Several students called out. Bruce and Benjamin, who were positioned opposite each other, separated by the length of the room, fired, hitting each other with the foam darts. Benjamin's gun was an automatic and held several darts, while Bruce's gun was mechanical and only held one at a time. As the students observed the difference—Bruce was only able to fire once while Benjamin had the ability to fire multiple times—they called out, "No, you need to be on the same side of the room!" And another called out, "You should only shoot once!"

"Oh, okay," Bruce said, crossing over to the board and picking up a piece of chalk. "So we need to make sure we are each only shooting one bullet and we are shooting from the same side of the room." He wrote these on the board, numbering them "1" and "2". "Anything else we need to do?"

A girl toward the front suggested, "You should mark the floor where they stand." Bruce wrote this down as well. "OK, let's have another trial. Count off!"

The students in the class yelled out, "3...2...1...FIRE!" Benjamin fired and a moment later, Bruce fired his gun.

"Noooo!" cried the students.

"You have to fire at the same time!" a student shouted.

"Oh, okay," said Bruce. He picked up the chalk again, wrote the third instruction, and continued, "So we gotta do this again!" The class groaned in response.

Bruce and the student aimed at the back board. The class once again counted down: "3...2...1...fire!!!" Once again Bruce and Benjamin each fired, but one of the darts did not discharge.

"Mr. C!" groaned one of the students. "Are you both using the same dart?"

"Hmmm," said Bruce, writing this new piece of information on the board. "We need the same kind of ammunition." He reloaded both guns. "OK...let's go again."

"3...2...1...FIRE!" Bruce and Benjamin fired again.

"Wait, who was watching to see where it landed? So we need someone to watch... so Curtis, go on to the back and see where it lands."

"3...2...1...FIRE!" They both fired. Curtis called out, "It was Benjamin! It was Benjamin!"

"OK," said Bruce, "Now we are talking. So what did we learn from that?"

"You have to write down the instructions," offered one student.

Bruce nodded. "And how long did that take?"

"A long time!"

"We had to do that like seven or eight times!"

"Right." Bruce began to erase the board as he talked. "So just to summarize— when you do an experiment, the first time it's always going to go wrong, and you are going to have to go back and modify it, and then you record your modifications and the new outcomes." Bruce began to erase the board. "OK, now we are going to switch gears. Malik, please draw a big bullseye on the board. We are going to discuss accuracy and precision. So if you are not sure what that is, we are going to see it right now."

This vignette draws attention to the student excitement and energy reverberating through the room as Bruce facilitated the activity. Characteristic of Bruce's classroom environment, the action happened lightning-fast, with students calling out different answers simultaneously and Bruce making split-second decisions as he progressed through the instructional period. Additionally, the vignette offers both positive and problematic insights into Bruce's practice. The demonstration was designed to generatively help students understand that experiments are repeated multiple times to streamline processes, and mistakes are both expected and necessary aspects of the learning process. Despite being a teacher-led activity, the lesson did involve all students, who actively participated, exhibited an edge-of-the-seat enthusiasm, and had fun (as evidenced by their laughter). Further, the creative employment of the Nerf gun collection in lieu of other science equipment showcases Bruce's capacity to make adaptation given the constraints of his context. The smooth flow of the activity and ease with which Bruce interacted with students also reflects the positive development of classroom relationships.

This account simultaneously demonstrates the characteristic, unstructured aspects of Bruce's teaching. While students found the demonstration to be exciting, no introduction was provided, no directions were given, and students did not follow the activity with any kind of formalized connection to science content other than quick Bruce's verbal summary (a surface connection to content). Bruce's pedagogy failed to attend to students who might have benefited from multiple ways of engaging the information, such as recording a summary or discussing the implications of the demonstration for scientific experiments, and in fact, some may not have fully processed the connection. Bruce could have provided other experimental science process connections, such as a link to the importance of specificity and objectivity of procedures, or referencing the steps of the scientific method. The demonstration, though exciting and experiential, was unstructured and provided only a cursory connection to content. Bruce limited the deep meaning-making of creating scientific procedures, and may not have ensured all his students understood the connection of the demonstration to the experimental process.

BECOMING-TEACHER

Bruce's processes of *becoming teacher*—his construction of teacher identity—occurred in relationship to his students, the conditions of his setting, and his own internal struggle between more traditional instruction and *teaching-differently*. With respect to his students, Bruce brought what he considered his authentic self to the classroom, wanting students to get to know him. He explained, "I get a lot of questions because I wear the yarmulke, I get a lot of questions about my collection of nerf guns, because they students are also interested in who you are, so showing them anything else, they would be able to sense it." He sought to infuse his lessons with his own hobbies, personal interests, and self-described "zany" characteristics

75

not only to personalize his teaching, but also to compensate for the lack of resources at his school. For example, class demonstrations and activities often revolved around his enormous personal collection of Nerf guns; he infused his fascination for SETI (Search for Extra-Terrestrial Intelligence) and space travel into class projects and discussions; he frequently discussed online gaming and technology with students during homeroom and study hall; and shared his love of theatre by facilitating an after-school drama club. Bruce believed bringing his "whole self" to teaching (Taylor & Coia, 2009) provided a non-typical learning experience for his students. He shared,

> This works to my favor, because there's always that zany teacher that you absolutely remember, the nutty one, like I don't believe that he brought Nerf guns to class. I don't believe that we just threw eggs across the playground. Or that he rolled a bowling ball at me. And it makes it memorable because it's so out there, it's not just a typical experience, and I think that's how my personality fits in there. The personalities, they can't be bland, I don't know any successful teachers who have bland personalities. Kids will find it boring and uninteresting.

Bruce also interpreted his teaching role more holistically than the norm: "I only see it partially as teaching them physics, a lot less than last year – I thought 'Oh, I teach physics.' It's a lot less teaching physics than being a guide, slash counselor, slash mentor, slash role model—it's a lot more of that, physics is just kind of the foot note." Because he saw his role as encompassing more than just his own physics classes, Bruce often broke through the norm of being bound to his own content area. For example, his roommate teacher was absent for nearly three weeks without leaving sufficient lessons for the students. When Bruce saw that students were not being occupied during this time, and the parade of substitute teachers were not providing any kind of useful structure for students, he volunteered to teach the classes until the teacher returned. This meant that Bruce taught nine periods in a row, which physically and mentally exhausted him, but he worried that without stepping in, the students might have missed out on several weeks of instruction.

Bruce positioned his students not just as the molar category of "students," but also as individuals with histories and who were at particular developmental stages in their lives. He commented, "[The students] are people, with their own lives and problems." Viewing being a teacher through such a holistic lens sometimes triggered responses that may have differed from the norm. For instance, Bruce was absent one Friday, and asked the substitute teacher to administer a quiz in his absence. When Bruce returned the following Monday, he found that the class had cheated on the quiz. Upon investigation, he discovered that the substitute teacher had left early, without notifying anyone at the school, leaving Bruce's students unattended. Taking the entire situation in account and acknowledging his students as individuals, Bruce decided to re-administer the quiz with no penalties. He commented,

Our day goes longer than the district day, so I guess [the substitute] passed out the work and then left…[they cheated] flagrantly. But I don't blame them. There was absolutely no supervision. That's why I'm letting them retake it and not just giving them all zeroes. I'm not going to blame ninth graders for acting like ninth graders.

The tensions (molar lines) within Bruce and in his setting conflicted with these individuations, or becoming-teacher processes, constructed in relation to his students—which may have explained some of the contradictions in his teaching and his communications about practice. For example, although Bruce strove to see his teaching as encompassing more than physics, or seeing his students as whole people, he stopped short of making his dissatisfaction with the school's harmful "zero-tolerance" policies known with the principal. His uncertainty about his position at the school and the new principal's evaluation of his teaching contributed to his becoming complacent—that is, his "not wanting to rock the boat" in terms of his instruction and feeling uncomfortable advocating for his students with the principal. This becoming represents a molar line that reproduces the common practice of teachers viewing their work as a-political and seeing themselves as lacking the ability to influence contexts and circumstances beyond the walls of the classroom (despite the reality that school, district, and state politics affect their decision-making and daily practice) (Thomas, 2013). Bruce explained,

There is that pressure, and it's not a small amount of pressure. In terms of the change between last year and this year, that's probably the biggest, even more than any pedagogical changes. The sheer, you know, these are your administrators, and they can lay you off. If they choose that physics is no longer appropriate for ninth grade, you're gone.

Bruce's preoccupation with survival in terms of retaining his position at the school conflicted with his classroom persona of a caring, zany teacher providing exciting learning experiences and reinforced two perennial molar lines in teaching – isolation within the school setting and the understanding of teaching work as apolitical. These factors contributed to uneven teacher-becomings that demonstrate the complexity of the processes involved in novice teachers' experience. At moments Bruce individuated his professional self as a humanizing and creative teacher, and others—particularly when he felt the pressure of the principal—he played the role of what he believed was a more traditional physics teacher.

SUMMARY

Bruce's case demonstrates the complexity of enacting a social justice-oriented or progressive pedagogy as a new teacher in a school environment with numerous constraints. In conjunction with his internal constraints, the enactment of a traditional pedagogy emerged along with the maintenance of long-held, traditional beliefs about teaching and learning, facilitating an internal struggle and tension with the inquiry-oriented and progressive approaches to teaching Bruce learned in his preservice preparation. The combination and interaction of the internal and external factors in his situation led him to proceed with much caution and to primarily err on the side of the "tested and true" traditional norms for classroom instruction, although occasional breaks from these norms did surface in his work. Bruce's case highlights that beginning teachers not only struggle in translating or bringing forth preservice learning into the novice years of teaching, but they also need to feel supported, mentored, and capable of taking risks in their teaching to break away from traditional, status quo pedagogies that fail to tap into students' background knowledge, differentiate for individual differences, or work towards social justice and equity. Without such support, teachers like Bruce, who began teaching with a conceptual knowledge base about equity-based and emergent teaching skills related to inquiry-based teaching, will struggle to enact these knowledge and practices in their classrooms.

Equitable, progressive, and social justice pedagogies are lines of flight that have the potential to reshuffle the molar norms of schooling. Bruce's case sheds light on the fits and starts that manifest as teachers seek to enact such pedagogies. Negotiations between and among internal and external constraints influence the ability to enact such modes of teaching. Thus, the construction and routine practice of enacting a pedagogy rooted in social justice is not likely to be smooth or easy, but rather, a difficult and convoluted process. The molar lines of Bruce's school environment presented challneges that diminished the capacity of working with students seamlessly to collectively generate critical questions about scientific phenomena. However, if enough lines of flight (and the right kinds of lines of flight) occur, these have the potential to feed back into the system create small shifts. Collectively, and over time, these shifts can transform systems of schooling as a whole, enabling unstriated, smooth space in which progressive, socially just, and equity centered teaching methods that break away from the status quo of teacher-centered instruction can be enacted.

DISRUPTING THE STATUS QUO THROUGH LINES OF FLIGHT

INTRODUCTION

In this chapter, we return to the concept of *assemblage* and build on the ideas introduced in the last chapter—molar, molecular, and *lines of flight*. We draw on these concepts as analytic tools to discuss the case of June, who taught tenth-grade biology in a self-contained special education setting in the same large urban district as Bruce and Mauro. In some ways, June's case seems very typical of the experiences of the first year teacher—she took on an assignment for which she was under-prepared (a special education biology position) in a school that had a reputation for being one of the most challenging in the city. Yet, in other ways, June's experience was atypical. For example, she had an abundance of professional support from her department chair and colleagues as well as very small classes. The way that June herself (her teacher multiplicity) came into composition with these elements – the *assemblage* they formed together – produced *lines of flight*, or breaks from the status quo, that interrupted multiple molar norms, including that of the dis-abled learner and the status quo of first-year teaching in an urban school.

As discussed in Chapter 4, an assemblage is a rhizomatic concept that refers to a multiplicity and the way its constituent parts mix or work together—that is, the way it functions as a substantive configuration. As the assemblage elements change, the nature of the assemblage and what it enables or inhibits changes as well. Thus, nothing exists nor operates in isolation, but rather, is constructed as and receives its meaning from the assemblage as a whole. By way of an example, Deleuze and Guattari (1987) describe two horses: the workhorse and the racehorse. Each of these, although they have the same animal element—a horse—are animated differently by the assemblages in which they function: the workhorse comes into composition with its blinders, its harness, its cart, the load it pulls, and produces slow, steady movements. The racehorse, on the other hand, is part of a mixture with a jockey, a racetrack, money or bets, and produces short bursts of speed. As discussed earlier in this book, an assemblage can also serve as an analytic tool for social phenomena like teaching. The students, the teacher, the classroom, the subject, the discourses present, the particular educational policies that are in vogue—these all work together to produce particular types of teaching. When these elements shift, or particular conditions are changed, the functions and productions—for example, the type of teaching practices that emerge—also *become-different*.

In terms of examining the functioning of an assemblage, we have also suggested that an analysis of its rhizomatic lines—or the molar and molecular lines that dictate how it works—is a fruitful method for parsing some of the complexities of the jointly-constituted practice of teaching. Molar lines refer to the rigid, normative forces that preserve the status quo. Also known as "overcoding," these lines may be imposed from the macro-level, such as institutional rules or societal control mechanisms, as well as internalized at the micro-level, as ways that we discipline ourselves, in the Foucauldian sense (Foucault, 1976). However, molar lines have very little power without supple, flexible molecular lines. Molecular lines are necessary for carrying out the work of the molar at the micro-level (Albrecht-Crane & Slack, 2003). Describing the entanglement and recursively reciprocal nature of the molar and molecular using the notions of *mass* and *class*, Deluze and Guattari (1987) contend, "The notion of mass is a molecular notion, operating according to a type of segmentation irreducible to the molar segmentarity of class. Yet classes are indeed fashioned from masses; they crystallize them. And masses are constantly flowing or leaking from classes" (p. 213).

When something does break free of the status quo—"something that flows or flees, that escapes the binary organizations, the resonance apparatus, and the overcoding machine" (Deleuze & Guattari, 1987, p. 216)—that *something* is called a *line of flight*. Lines of flight are lines of creation, mutation, of transformation, of *becoming*. These lines provide a momentary escape, interruption, or eruption, a temporal deterritorialization of the norm or undermining of stoppages. Lines of flight in the classroom might be any subversive or creative act—the use of statistics on local poverty levels to teach a lesson on mathematical proportions, an unexpected student question, or even a loud laugh during a quiet test. Notably, although lines of flight are productive, they are not necessarily productive of something good or positive. In addition, every deterritorialization must necessarily include a reterritorialization—a recapturing by the control apparatus—because they are entangled with the molar: "Molecular escapes and movements would be nothing if they did not return to the molar segments to reshuffle their segments, their binary distributions of sexes, classes, and parties" (pp. 216–217). Yet, as these lines of flight are reterritorialized by the molar—the bell rings and students leave the class for the day, the teacher must plan another lesson according to a particular objective—change has occurred, the "reshuffle [of] segments" referred to in the quote above. In this way, lines of flight operate as a change mechanism for society or social phenomena. Indeed, "it is along this line of flight that things come to pass, becomings evolve, revolutions take shape" (Deleuze, 1995, p. 45).

In the following chapter, we use two main concepts—*assemblage* and *lines of flight*—to discuss the way that June, her students, and her contextual elements worked together to produce several important disruptions, or lines of flight, throughout the term of this study, including inquiry-based teaching and student advocacy. We suggest that, from continuously constructing these multiple lines of flight, June and her students engaged in an interruption of several molar categories and discourses. This includes that of the isolated, struggling first year teacher; the autonomous, ideal learner; and the deficient special education student. Below, we discuss major elements of June's multiplicity, and describe the way these worked together to produce these disruptions from the status quo of teaching in high-poverty, urban schools and exclusionary settings like special education.

JUNE AND WASHINGTON HIGH SCHOOL

June was twenty-four, White, and female. She possessed a funky sense of style, wearing her hair in an asymmetrical pixie cut with pink highlights. She sported a nose ring and had colorful tattoos peeking out of the bottom of her sleeves. Although she grew up in what she referred to as "white suburbia," June said she was always interested in science and environmental justice. Despite originally intending to attend school to become a dentist, due to an error in application processing on the part of the dental school, June found herself instead applying on a whim to the NUTR program. She embraced the community aspects of the program, crediting the relational aspect with a good part of her success, developing close relationships with several other residents.

Although she completed her residency year with success, program faculty were concerned when they learned that June planned to accept a position at Washington High School to teach special education biology. Washington had a reputation for being one of the most challenging schools in the city, notorious for outbreaks of violence and chaotic classrooms. In addition, June would be the only NUTR graduate at her school site—whenever possible, the program tried to place graduates at least in pairs so they could support each other during their first year of teaching. June herself was initially hesitant to accept the position, but after she met with the new principal, the science department chair, and the other special education science teachers, she was convinced that Washington would be the best place for her.

June's own beliefs about teaching aligned with the NUTR program's teaching philosophy. She explained, "I really bought into [the NUTR pedagogy], like all of it, from my core." She aimed to infuse all lessons with an investigation or exploratory component as well as opportunities for students to collaborate in meaning making. She described her goal for each lesson as "To get them to work together, to try to investigate this phenomenon, then from there to lead into some sort of understanding of the phenomenon…and then for them to produce something, at the end, using their new knowledge." June also hoped to make her classes interesting and active, with "students moving around and discussing with each other and able to talk about content."

PRACTICES CO-PRODUCED BY AN ASSEMBLAGE

In analyzing the function of the overall teaching-assemblage of which June was a part, we noticed that multiple practices emerged aligning with those she learned in her preservice program. These included inquiry-based teaching, differentiating for multiple needs, and reframing assessments. These practices were consistent with her stated beliefs and intentions regarding instruction—for example, June commented in her first interview, "I am always trying, to whatever lesson I make, to do something that is inquiry-based, to have some sort of investigation, and so far I haven't had one class where that isn't the case." Following the last lesson in her full unit, June again emphasized, "I try as much as possible to get [inquiry] into every lesson. Something where [students] don't know what they are doing at first, but they are going to figure it out, and hopefully they are going to figure it out on their own." Indeed, nearly every class contained some investigative component, ranging from short "do-now" explorations to experimental labs requiring students to pose questions and hypothesize about phenomena, collect and analyze data, draw conclusions, and share their findings. For example, when learning about the properties of water molecules, students conducted an experiment demonstrating concepts of adhesion and cohesion by collecting water droplets on the head of a penny. June provided students with a graphic organizer that guided students through the processes of the scientific method. With June's guidance, students created hypotheses for a common question—"How many water droplets fit on the head of a penny?"—and conducted three trials, averaging the results and recording the data. Next, June posed an additional question: "Will you get more or less drops [of water] on your penny if you dip it in dish detergent?" Students repeated the procedure with their pennies dipped in dish soap. After recording their data, June helped them create a graph to visually display the data, and asked them to theorize about what had happened.

June's classroom at times simulated the rhizome, offering multiple entryways to students (Deleuze & Guattari, 1987) into the lesson or content. June was purposeful in the planning of her class period, ensuring that each ninety-minute period had as multiple modalities of learning and as many supports as possible. Each activity was accompanied by some sort of guiding organizer, visual materials, and hands-on tasks or manipulatives, and students were often presented with different forms of media. Having multiple forms of representation and several activities planned also enabled June to adapt her teaching to support her students' learning needs. In one instance, June had designed an interactive video assignment, asking students to use a graphic organizer to identify information in the video. She instructed students to notify her to pause the video when one of the topics arose. However, the students declined to participate. After stopping the video a few times herself, she cut the activity short and moved into the next piece, an experiential lab. After the lesson, June reflected, "I saw that I was losing them…I immediately saw like, they were either too tired or, I need to do something where they are being active."

June also adjusted her lessons specifically for the needs of each class. She articulated, "Some classes have assignments that others don't...there are different types of learners and needs." At times this meant adjusting the content and teaching methods, such as in the case of her fifth block, B day class—a class of five boys—where she modified her lessons to allow her to actually sit with them in a group and work alongside them. She commented, "We move through material slower, so I've definitely cut out pieces with them, but I've tried not to cut out anything significant, I think." Although her lessons may have varied from class to class, she reflected, "I see that each class plays out differently, but yet they are all accomplishing the same goal."

As conscious as she was about her teaching and her students as learners, June was also aware of how her students interpreted their own abilities, strengths, and needs as students and individuals. She understood that many of her students had internalized the label of "special needs" and had very low confidence in their abilities to handle certain academic tasks, often resulting in "shutting down" or refusing to complete assignments, especially summative assessments. When this occurred, June sought to find other ways to help the student, either by modifying the assignment, reframing her questions, or scaffolding their work in some way. For example, when students were unable to complete an assessment that asked for the definition of terms relating to the scientific method, June wrote the definitions on a sheet of paper and asked them to match the terms to them. On another assessment, a student balked at writing a detailed answer to a prompt asking students to describe how a video about euthanasia related to bioethics. June realized that the problem was not an issue of not knowing the answer, but rather the students' lack of confidence in his ability to express himself in writing. She shared,

> [He wrote] 'Yes, it is bioethics because it's about a man who's very sick and wants to die.' So I said, 'Can you give me more, like what are your thoughts on it? And he was like, 'I can't.' And I was like, 'What if you tell me, and I write it?' And he's like, 'OK.' And this is word for word what he said, and I'm not even kidding: 'There is no cure. He can't move anything on his body. If he lives, he will suffer more. But if he dies he will be in peace with no pain. He should be allowed to die.' And I looked at him, and I was like... 'What you said was beautiful.' And he was like, 'Really?' And I was like, 'Yeah.' And I was like, 'Let's work on, we'll do this, but let's work on bits and pieces of getting you to be able to express your thoughts.' And he was like, 'OK,' and I saw emotion from him, like sincere emotion, for the first time.

In finding ways to meet each students' needs, working with them at their current level of ability and helping them slowly bridge to required skills and competencies (Cochran-Smith, 2004), June and her students constructed lines of flight that disrupted the molar category of "special needs student" who was unsuccessful at "regular" academic tasks.

June's use of alternate forms of assessment and her attitude toward testing further broke from the status quo in multiple ways. Her students' low confidence toward taking tests were interrupted as they experienced success, experiencing types of assessment that differed from the norm of formal multiple choice formatting. Eventually her students outperformed their Biology peers on common assessments, disrupting the very binary categories of general education/special education student. June worked to facilitate such assessment experiences early. In the beginning of the year, she planned her very first assessment as a "practicum," which she explained entailed students moving from station to station, completing various activities: watching a video on June's iphone and completing a related prompt; identifying objective and subjective statements; selecting photos to identify characteristics of living and non-living things; and using a set of provided materials to design an experiment. Prior to the assessment, she explained, "They are not going to know it's an assessment, until they are done. And then I'm just going to tell them that they just took their test."

During the actual assessments, June negotiated with students, constantly encouraging them and redirecting them when they became tired or disengaged. Her small classes seemed to be an enabling factor in being able to interact with every student during an assessment to help them finish. For example, during an assessment on graphing, one student laid her head down on the desk, splaying out her arms, her pencil rolling across the table. June came over and sat down next to her. "Come on [student's name]," June said in a low voice, indicating the passage where the student had left off. "Let's read this together. Read the first sentence to me?"

June sought to enable her students to demonstrate their learning not only on assessments she created, but also those required by the school and district. For example, the science department had mandated a series of common assessments, which June called "CRTs" (Criterion Referenced Tests). Periodically, every student was required to take these tests, which measured scientific skills such as graphing and familiarity with common scientific terms. Although June was required to enter these tests as a grade, she told her students that she would count every problem that was attempted, whether it was right or not. Once the stakes were removed, June believed, "The students actually try."

NEGOTIATING WITH STUDENTS

One enabling element of June's teaching-assemblages was the size of her classes. She taught five classes per day, each with no more than five students, which is unusual for a school in an urban setting. The small size of each class allowed June to get to know her students and develop connections with them that ultimately facilitated learner-centered, inquiry based instruction. June's students, all of whom were students of color, had been labeled as "special education" students and judged to be unable to be educated in a mainstream setting. From the beginning of the school year, June recognized that students were reluctant to engage in her instructional activities, which she theorized stemmed from students' self-doubting of their academic abilities. To secure their participation in her lessons, June "came into composition" with her students in various ways—including building relationships with them, offering frequent encouragement, using incentives, and engaging in one-on-one negotiations.

June was aware that her students were considered "problem" students by other teachers and had internalized their "special needs" label. She wanted to communicate her caring and respect to students as a way to engage them productively in her class and acknowledge that they were more than the label of "special education" student. She described, "I'm trying to build a relationship where I respect my students, and instead of trying to motivate them with…a negative…[I'm] trying to tell them that they are intelligent, and capable, students and people, and that's why I want you to work hard, not because I say so and you need to do it." June displayed her caring by "checking in" with students and making it clear to that she was interested in their overall wellbeing. If students had their heads on their desks or were otherwise disengaged, she made sure they were feeling okay before gently asking them to re-engage in the activity at hand. Rather than assuming students' intent, she explained, "one of the biggest deals…[is] making an effort to reach out to kids on a personal level and figuring out…what their background is, and why they are depressed, and that's going to help you in the long run."

June also deliberately provided encouragement to students to bolster their confidence, expressing her belief that they were more than capable of the work involved in her lessons and referring to their intellectual capacity. Prior to an activity, June might tell students, "OK, I need all your brainpower for this," or "I need your intelligence here." If a student became frustrated or disengaged during a lesson, June would reinforce her belief in them: "I know you can do it," or "Stop acting like you're not smart." When students completed their task, it was not unusual for June to wrap up by saying something like, "See, I told you, you are geniuses!" She also deliberately likened their work to scientists: "The reason we are doing this…scientists always graph their data." Or: "OK, the last thing I want you to do, we have to do some writing because we are scientists and we have to write up our conclusions." By positioning students this way, June was creating lines of flight away from the molar category of "special education student," and students, at least temporarily, engaged in becoming-geniuses and becoming-scientists.

The small size of her classes enabled June to engage in the kind of one-on-one negotiations that she might not have been able to in a larger class. For example, during one observation, students were required to complete a school-wide assessment. As June handed out the tasks, one student laid her head on her desk and said, "I don't want to do this!" June said, "I know, but you'll do it anyway." When the student still did not move, June squatted next to her desk. "You are too smart not to do this. Come on, the first one isn't hard at all. What is it asking?" The student picked up her pencil and began working. A few minutes later, a different student put her pencil aside and took out her phone. When June asked her if she was done, the student shook her head. June crouched down again and began coaching her through the next question. "Come on, you are almost done. Did you read this one? What does it say?" The student did not respond, so June sat in the chair next to her and began to read the question to her. The student pointed at the answer, and June nodded. "OK, now you are done!"

As June spent more time with her students, she began to tailor her negotiation strategies, as her students did not all respond the same way. For example, she learned that "[Student's name] responds really well to being successful. So if she feels she's doing a really good job, or that she's really smart, she'll keep pushing herself." For this student, June kept up a constant stream of encouragement throughout class sessions, and often sent positive text messages to the girl's mother. Another student needed to be in constant motion, and June often tapped him to be her assistant so he could move around the room, draw on the board, and work with other students. Describing her strategy, June noted, "He can't help it, he needs to be moving... So who did I have at the board the entire time? [Student's name]. Can you write this, can you draw this, can you do this?"

THE M&M EXPERIMENT

Four students sat facing the front of the room. At one table, Lydia and Tyrone were paired, and at the other, Jose and Miguel would be working together. June handed each of the students a copy of a graphic organizer that scaffolded each of the steps in the scientific method.

"I'm giving you a new worksheet. What should be the first thing you do?" she asked.

Three students answered in unison, their practiced reply indicating this was a familiar question. "Name and date at the top!" they exclaimed.

June nodded affirmatively, then called out to one of the students, Tyrone, as she held out three clear plastic cups stacked one on top of another. "Can I give you a task?" Tyrone nodded. "Can you put water in these three cups?" Tyrone obligingly took the cups and went to the sink at the back of the room to fill them.

"OK, I'm coming around," June announced to the other students, grabbing a large bag of "fun-size" packets of M&Ms from the front lab table. "OK, I'm going to put the M&M's..." As she placed one of the small packets of M&M's on a table next to a student's paper, the student immediately picked up the bag and ripped it open. June cautioned, "If I see you eating them, it's over."

"But why!?" said another student, Jose.

"Because she might let us eat them later," his partner, Miguel, replied.

"Miguel knows me so well!" June explained. "The reason is that you have to use them first for the experiment."

At that moment, the two students at the opposite table began talking loudly. June leaned back against her desk and crossed her arms, staring at them expectantly until they noticed her stern look. As the talking faded, June asked, "Can we listen to instructions?"

Miguel said, "Yes."

"OK then. I'm going to come around and place one bag of M&Ms next to your paper. Do not eat them."

Tyrone returned from the back of the room balancing the three cups of water. "I need a cup at each table, quickly," She told him. As he set the cups down in front of the other student, she continued: "What I would like you to do first..." She stopped her instruction as some of the students began talking again. "I'm being serious right now. You are taking advantage of me."

"Come on, Ms. L," said one of the students, Lydia. "We got this."

"All right, what I need you to do—open your pack of M&Ms, but only to look at them." She then drew the students' attention to the graphic organizer she had distributed, holding it up and indicating the first question. "In the first box, what does it say, Miguel?"

"Make observations."

"OK, so what I want in that box is objective observations about what you have in front of you." She paused for a moment. "Should anyone write, 'M&M's'?"

"No," answered Miguel.

"OK, good." The door opened and a student entered, having just returned from the restroom. June said, "Someone tell Ashley what we are doing, quickly."

"You aren't to eat the M&Ms." Lydia told Ashley. "You can only look at them."

Directing Ashley to a seat to work with Tyrone and Lydia, June said, "OK, so right now you need three objective observations." She waited a few moments while students started writing, and then began to check on students' work.

As June approached the group of three students, at the other table, Jose called out, "I'm done!"

She stopped immediately and walked over to Jose's table instead, glancing at his paper and seeing that he had three sentences written down about the M&M's. "What about your teammate?" She asked, referring to Miguel, who looked up and shook his head. June continued, "So together, I need you to have three objective observations." She moved over to the other side of the table and saw that Miguel did not have anything written yet. He made no move, but continued to stare at the M&Ms on his desk. June tapped her finger next to the M&Ms and asked him, "So as a scientist, what do you see?" Miguel did not reply, so she squatted down to get closer to the student's level. He murmured an answer softly. "Good, keep going with that thought," June encouraged him.

She turned back to the rest of the students. "OK, so if you have done the first step, what I want you to do now...what is the second step of the scientific method?"

"Questions!" called a student.

"OK. To ask some questions. So what I want you to do is put down some questions you could ask." She stopped and a few seconds went by before she asked students to give her an example of a question they could ask about the M&Ms they had in front of them. "So what's one question?"

Several students offered ideas. "Why are all my M&Ms different colors?" asked Lydia.

"How many M&Ms are in a bag?" inquired Jose.

Tyrone called out, "Why are there M's on the outside?"

"OK," said June, "Let's see if we can come up with a question that involves the materials you have- the water and the M&Ms."

"Why are we putting M&M's into the water?" Lydia offered.

"OK, now how can you make that into a question you can investigate right now?" June countered. "Write it down." After a moment she walked over to check on the other table. To the two boys working together, she admonished, "I see no questions. I see written-on fingers and chapstick, but no questions."

One of the boys said, "What would happen if we put the M&Ms in the water?"

June smiled and said to the class at large, with obvious pleasure, "All right! We're starting to think like scientists, you guys!" She turned back to the two boys. "OK, so what would you predict would happen if you did an experiment with this question?"

"It might change color?" Miguel suggested.

"OK, write that down. Now, Jose," June continued, "Why don't you come up with a second prediction, and then you share." June crossed to the other table, where the Ashley and Lydia sat chatting, having completed their first step. "Your task is an individual one right now," June told them. "You come up with a prediction"—she turned to Ashley—"then YOU come up with a prediction, and then you share."

June returned to the other table with the two boys. "OK, now I want you to actually do it," she said to them, meaning they should drop the M&Ms in the water. "Don't put all of them in the water, because then you can't eat them later." She watched as the students each dropped a handful of M&Ms into the cup. Swirls of color immediately appeared as the bright candy coating began to dissolve into the water.

"OK, now put your observations on the back," she prompted the two boys, referring to the other side of the graphic organizer. She crossed back to the other table, repeating her instructions with the second group.

Returning to the first table, she read what one of the pair of boys had written on their graphic organizers. "I like this," she told him, tapping on one of the lines of text he had written. She said to the class again, "I see a lot of observations here! Scientists make a lot of observations."

After another moment of students writing, June said, "So the next step after you make your observations is to flip your paper. I need you to be looking at the explanation box. What I want you to tell me—and this is your exit ticket—is to tell me, why did whatever happen, happen? So the observations you made, WHY did that happen? Don't REPEAT for me what happened. I want to know WHY. OK, so Miguel, tell me what I want you to do?"

"We are supposed to be writing why the water turned colors."

"Yep. OK, there are four minutes left in class, and you are going to need all of those four minutes. So tell me why it happened—don't tell me WHAT, tell me WHY."

After students had handed in their exit tickets, one asked, "Can we eat the M&Ms?"

"Yes. And you have to drink the colored water," June joked.

"EWWW!" Exclaimed one of the girls. One of the boys tipped back his glass, pretending to drink.

"I'm just kidding," June quickly said. "Don't drink it, because it's sink water." As students munched happily on their M&Ms, June told them, "And don't tell your next period teacher who gave you the candy."

The bell sounded, and students shuffled out the door. June called out to Miguel, and he turned around at the sound of his name. June approached him. She indicated that she wanted to check in with him about an incident that had occurred earlier in the class period. "I care about you," June began. "But I also care about your grades. What happened to your leg?"

The student pulled his pant leg up slightly to show her a small scratch he had been complaining about during class. She made a face at him, saying, "Suck it up!" She laughed as she saw him out the door.

This vignette provides an example of the type of teaching that June often accomplished. In this instance, by "coming into composition" with her students and providing high levels of support, she was able to scaffold interactive learning activities requiring high-level thinking skills in which students successfully engaged. This particular activity, although seemingly simple, supported students through key, open-ended scientific practices appropriate for any tenth grade biology class. Students made objective observations of the materials they had available—a packet of M&Ms and a cup of water—and formulated a question that they could investigate using those materials. Given these materials and their observed properties, students predicted what they thought might happen when they dropped the M&Ms in the water, and observed the results. Students then had to offer a possible explanation for what happened to the M&Ms once they were immersed in the water. Given the status quo functioning of high-poverty urban classrooms—much less ones in which the students are labeled as 'special needs'—these activities serve as lines of flight that disrupt both the type of teacher-led, watered down lessons usually observed in such settings as well as normalized expectations of what such students are capable of accomplishing.

During the lesson, some of the ways June worked together with her students to ensure their participation were apparent—for example, when Miguel was reluctant in the beginning to write down an observation about the M&Ms, June approached him, crouched down to speak with him face to face, and accepted his verbal answer first before validating him and then directing him to write his answer down. In another example, she also immediately involved Tyrone in the activity by requesting he fill the cups with water. Tyrone's ability to concentrate was tested by his need for movement. By acknowledging this need and simultaneously giving him an important job that was necessary to start the lesson, June successfully engaged Tyrone in the activity.

The relationships that June and her students forged also clearly affected their work together. For instance, when June commented that her students were taking advantage of her, Lydia responded with '*We got this, Ms. L!*' indicating her, and her peers', willingness to continue with the activity. Throughout the lesson, June also subtly demonstrated that she believed her students were capable of completing the lesson, positioning them as *scientists ("We are starting to think like scientists, you guys!")* who observed, hypothesized, and made meaning of phenomena, rather than students who had been taken out of their regular classroom settings because they were not able to complete the same academic tasks as other students. In this way, these interactions were lines of flight that cracked the molar category of "special needs student," and at least in that moment, students experienced a *becoming-scientist.*

OTHER ASSEMBLAGE ELEMENTS

In examining June's case from the outset, the deck seemed stacked against her: a brand new teacher, teaching a population of students for which she was not prepared, without a resident partner, and in a school with an infamous reputation for being a challenging professional environment. However, an analysis of the factors working to collectively produce her teaching shows that many elements, both personal and environmental, contributed to creating enabling conditions for teaching and otherwise working with students in ways that broke entrenched patterns of urban education. For instance, June herself brought several qualities shown to enable success for novice teachers, including a positive attitude and enthusiasm toward teaching (Hebert & Worthy, 2001; Tait, 2008), a reflective disposition (Bianchini & Cazavos, 2007), commitment and motivation (Eldar et al., 2003; Luft & Roehrig, 2005) and a tendency to take initiative and self-advocate (Starkey, 2010; Ulvik, Smith, & Helleve, 2009). In terms of her classes, June believed she had "drawn the long straw." She only taught one content area, and as previously noted, each of her classes was very small, which allowed her to gain in-depth knowledge of her students' backgrounds and academic and socio-emotional needs. This knowledge, in turn, both assisted her in planning appropriately-supported lessons and forging connections with her students that increased their likelihood of participating in more active, learner-centered lessons.

In addition to the factors that June brought as part of her own teacher-multiplicity and the productive relationships June constructed with her students, she also had multiple layers of support that contributed to the lines of flight constructed in her first year. In particular, she had a mentor and advocate in the form of her department chair, was part of a collaborative science teacher community, and was close with another teacher. These all served as supports to mediate the isolation and pedagogical struggle new teachers often face, and which create molar conditions that tend to reinforce transmission teaching and authoritarian classroom power struggles, as well as perpetuate high rates of novice teacher attrition.

Although June's actual school-based mentor was not helpful, June's department chair unofficially stepped into the role early in the year. June described her department chair as "amazing," and related that she would help June think through and refine her lessons and assessments. "She actually looks at our lesson plans, and gives positive critiques…she'll look at my tests and tells me things that she thinks would work. She's been nothing but positive and giving me really good feedback." In addition, June's department chair had established weekly professional learning community (PLC) meetings, and encouraged the teachers to collaborate together on lessons. June reported that she had "really built a bond with some of the teachers," especially another new Chemistry teacher with whom she often worked.

PROCESSES OF BECOMING-TEACHER

June's situated processes of identity development, or *teacher-becomings,* were constructed in relation to her students, their responses, and the various enabling and constraining conditions of her setting. Within her assemblage, June developed as a caring teacher, but also one who held her students to very high standards and came to believe their "disability" did not hinder their success—they merely required different pathways through curriculum and academic processes. While in the first interview June discussed her students' issues with communicating and information-processing as drawbacks, by the final interview, she was convinced her students were just as capable as "general education" students. She described her students' label as "special needs bullshit," arguing, "I am pushing them just as hard as I would push kids that weren't special needs and they are doing it just as well – it's just structuring it in a different way." This transformation in the ways June viewed her students demonstrates a major break from the status quo regarding special needs students in schools. Often, students with a *special needs* or *disabled* label are viewed as inferior because they do not fit neatly into the entrenched norm of *student as autonomous learner*. Yet, from her day-to-day interactions with her students, June began to realize that they were not *less than* because they required supports, merely *different.* By teaching in ways that differed from the norm and were tailored to meet their needs, her students could indeed be both different and high-achieving.

In relation to her students, June enacted a situated identity as a caring teacher in both explicit and implicit ways. In one of our interviews, she explained,

> I hope I'm really seen as a teacher who cares. You know, I care about the content, I love my subject area, so I hope that comes off to my students, and also that I really care about them being successful…I'll bend over backwards

to make sure you are successful, but also that you need to put in the effort too, but in the end, that's making you more of a successful person. So I've said that in numerous ways, and I think a lot of the students have gotten it.

To demonstrate that she cared about her students, June would often soften a redirection with a statement referring to her feelings about them—for example, when a student resisted June's attempts to refocus her during a lesson, June said, "I'm only pushing you like this because I care." As shown in the first vignette of this chapter, June asked a male student who had been distracted during the lesson to stay afterward and talk with her. During their discussion, June sought to communicate that she cared about him as a person as well as how he performed in her class. She told him, "I care about you, but I also care about your grades."

She also indicated her caring indirectly by recognizing that her students were human beings with needs, instead of seeing them as only academic bodies that should function to complete academic tasks. She kept snacks like granola bars and graham crackers in the room in case they were hungry, and had a Brita water filter that she used to keep clean water for thirsty students. June showed her understanding of physical discomfort as well. One morning, a student entered the classroom after the bell had rung, going straight to the fan, holding her shirt away from her body and fanning herself. Rather than admonishing the student to sit and begin working on the lesson, June said, "So after you cool off, go ahead and get started." With these small acts, acknowledging the students' basic needs for food, water, and physical comfort served as a line of flight escaping the status quo of ignoring the body in favor of the rational brain in schools (Zembylas, 2007).

Students responded positively to June's repeated words and actions demonstrating her caring, which reinforced her identity formation processes. Over the semester, students began spending more and more time in June's room, choosing to spend their lunch periods there rather than the cafeteria with their peers. Students also began coming to June for comfort. For example, during one observation, a student who had been accidentally left behind at the school for a field trip came crying to June's room, interrupting the lesson and telling June she needed to talk. Although she was being observed by her department chair, June stopped the lesson, enfolded the student in a quick hug, and let her know she would talk to her as soon as she got to a stopping point.

Over the first several months of school, June also became more confident in her role as an authority figure who sought to provide calm, orderly leadership in the classroom but avoid control (Freire, 1998). She explained, "I'm never going to be this, aggressive authoritative figure, but ... I still want to be an authority." June was committed to remaining calm and level-headed in the classroom at all times, having experienced the unproductive results that occurred the year before when she had become angry with students in classroom situations. In her first interview, she articulated, "I don't, like, let my blood boil, which is something I did in the beginning of last year...I've like, made a promise to myself, that nothing is personal against me." Part of her learning included how to resolve tensions between her desire to cultivate an open environment conducive to generative learning, but still be able to lead the class. She worried that if her students saw her as "too chill," they might not heed her instructions if a serious situation occurred. She wondered,

[Will there] come a time when something happens in my room and I can't – now that I've shown I'm not this aggressive person you need to listen to, in that manner, that I'm not going to like, handle it properly? …or they won't take me seriously?

However, as she saw that students did respond well to her calm persona and other qualities, her worries that she was only "gliding along luckily" began to dissipate. As an example, she described her last class of the day, five boys who had a reputation outside her classroom for being extremely challenging. She explained, "But the thing is, I'm seeing that those boys do take me seriously, they stop cursing when I ask them to stop cursing, that they apologize for what they are doing, and they are like, 'only for you.'"

June's small classes, relationships with her students, and department support contributed to an environment where she felt safe to become an advocate for her students as another part of her identity multiplicity. This occurred subtly—for example, in providing classroom pathways for success that escaped the status quo of "disabled" student—but she also advocated for her students in more direct ways. The case of Tyrone provides an illumination of this becoming-teacher process. Tyrone was one of June's most challenging students from the beginning—his behavior was unpredictable, and his frequent absences complicated June's efforts to build a relationship and learn what he might respond to in terms of negotiation strategies. During a lab investigating the concepts of cohesion and adhesion, June was thrilled to see Tyrone participating and engaged, working with a partner to test the amount of water droplets that fit on the head of a penny. The class was interrupted by the head of "In-School Suspension" (ISS), a sort of holding facility for students who had done something which merited being removed from class, but was not egregious enough for an actual out-of-school suspension. The ISS head told June he needed to take Tyrone, and asked that he bring his work with him. Dismissing the student to go without questioning the school authority would have upheld the status quo of segregation and exclusion of special education students by removing Tyrone from his already segregated special education classroom. It would have also reinforced the molar category of the student as worthy of punishment, the "Bad" student. However, June reacted differently. She told the authority they were in the middle of an experiment, which the student could not take with him. After initially balking, the authority was eventually swayed by her argument and agreed that she would bring the student down to him after class was concluded.

In the larger school context, June also became a leader within her department. The teachers in the science department met once a week in June's classroom for collaboration as a "professional learning community" (PLC), and over time, as June shared her inquiry-based lessons and ideas in the PLC meetings, teachers began to come to her for advice. June credited her year with the NUTR as a contributing factor, commenting,

> [the NUTR experience] obviously shapes my instruction, and just puts me ahead of other teachers. I mean, I'm not saying I'm better, but it gives me advantages over a lot of first AND second year teachers I have been working with. And it's really evident, because I've already had a lot of teachers come to me for stuff that I'm doing, or help with their lesson… But I've had veteran teachers come, again, not like promoting myself, but just because of what I learned in that year, where they had just been introduced to it in their staff development days.

June quickly became considered an expert within her department, the "go-to" person for inquiry-based and experiential lessons. June's department chair, who also participated in the PLC meetings, observed June's facility with planning and enacting these type of lessons, and asked her to lead a professional development session about inquiry-based teaching methods.

Being positioned as an expert and leader of inquiry-based instruction is a line of flight cutting across multiple normative boundaries. "Expert" or "leader" is a position not often available to beginning teachers, as the hierarchical, molar lines of schools usually relegate new educators to a powerless and voiceless novice position (Saka, Southerland, & Brooks, 2009; Scherff, 2008). Bolstered by her year of inquiry-based teacher preparation, an open and collaborative teaching community, and a sense of success in enacting inquiry-based practices, June pursued a line of flight escaping this oppressive norm, which over time, led to increased professional confidence. June began to take initiative to lead other efforts, such as proposing to lead a school-wide project to identify common roots, affixes, and suffixes of disciplinary vocabulary among the core classes and collaborate with the teachers to use them to create linguistic supports for students across the grade level. She also felt comfortable and secure in, at times, becoming the voice of dissent within her department. As an illustration, June took issue with a department-wide assessment of science skills, arguing that the assessment was inappropriate for her students and should have been collaboratively planned with input from all science teachers. Although she unhappily administered the first assessment to her students, she was able to convince her department chair to allow her to modify the assessment format to meet her students' needs and provide accommodations as needed.

A second line of flight is evident in the disruption of the molar line of teacher socialization patterns (Achinstein, Ogawa, & Speiglman, 2005; Allen, 2009; Zeichner & Gore, 1990). Rather than the norm of rigid veteran educators inducting a new teacher into entrenched norms of traditional instruction and isolation within the school community, the teachers in the science department at Washington, from June's perspective, were open to collaboration and eager to learn inquiry-based teaching methods. These lines of flight, reconstructed in weekly PLC meetings and in June's other interactions with her colleagues, not only interrupted the norm of teacher socialization, but supported the emergence of different patterns of teaching as well as June's teacher-becomings as a confident leader and advocate within the school.

THE CRITERION-REFERENCED TEST

June was clearly annoyed, her frustration palpable as she paced in front of her classroom. As I (Katie) set up my computer, she walked over and sat next to me, letting me know that her plans for the day had changed. "So we're not actually going to do the lesson today, except for the last thirty minutes, maybe," she said. "We have to take a criterion-referenced test. All the science classes have to take it." She went on to explain that the test had been written by another first year teacher in the department, who she described as "A TFA'er [Teach for America] who wants to go to medical school." June herself hadn't been allowed to give any input into what would go on the test or how it was constructed. She thought that if all the science teachers had to give it to their students, the entire department should have created the test collaboratively, or at a minimum, the teachers should have been able to provide feedback once the test was created.

She showed me a copy of the original test, and pointed out the tiny print, the number of questions that had been crammed onto one page, and the advanced vocabulary. "Just by giving [the students] an assessment that looks complicated, they break down," she explained. Concerned that the test would be daunting for her students and they would not even attempt it, she went to the department head with requests for accommodations. Her supervisor had conceded to enlarging the print and expanding the test into three pages, as well as agreeing to extra time, but those were the only allowances. However, June confessed that she also planned to read the questions to them and paraphrase if necessary, as she felt the vocabulary was at a higher level than most of her students could read. With her face set in a grim line, she declared, "I'm reading it to them and I don't give a shit. It's a shitty test. And I'm telling them that I didn't make it and I'm sorry they have to take it."

June was not exaggerating. The first words out of her mouth to her students when the bell rang: "So don't get mad at me. I'm going to preface with that." She held up the papers containing the assessment, continuing, "This is a science assessment, and everyone has to take it. It's graded, but it's graded on how hard you work on each section. I didn't make it, nor did I want you to take it." She emphasized, "Don't get overwhelmed by this- I know there's some things on here we haven't covered yet." She then explained the purpose to them. "The purpose of it is to read something"— she tapped on one of the passages of text on the first sheet of the assessment—"and then answer questions about it. Or, if there is data"—she pulled open the second page, showing them the set of problems there—"They want you to graph it."

She began passing the tests out. As she did, she reminded her students forcefully, "All of you are capable of doing this." She then clarified, "If you want me to read

95

something to you, I will do that. If you want to know what something means, I'll do that for you too." She walked back up to her desk and asked them to get started, but none of the students moved to pick up their pencils and begin. She told them, "The sooner we finish this, the sooner we can move on." Lydia laid her head down on the table and groaned, "I don't want to DO this!"

June replied, "I know, but you'll do it anyway." To all three students, she reminded them, "I don't want to give you guys this test, but I have to." She crossed over to where Lydia sat, crouching down so they were on the same level, and looked her in the eye. "You are too smart not to do this," June told her in a matter-of-fact tone. She pointed to the first problem. "Come on, the first one isn't hard at all. What is it asking?" With a sigh, Lydia picked up her pencil and began to work without replying.

During the remainder of the test, June rotated between the three students, encouraging them to continue. When Ashley put down her pencil and took out her phone, June walked over and asked her if she was finished. When Ashley shook her head, June advised, "Why don't you take a short break and then try again?" The student looked away. "I don't want to." June looked at her paper, gesturing to her nearly-complete test. "Come on, you are almost done. Did you read this last one? What does it say?" When the student didn't respond, June began to read the passage to her quietly. Once she had finished, the student pointed at the answer. "OK," June said, "Now write that down and you are done!"

After class, June felt proud that each student finished the test, though some had needed repeated encouragement. She told me, "I think they actually did well on it. I mean, Lydia, it was like pulling teeth. But, when she realized, like the questions were not that hard, and she could answer them, it was just like annoying, which I agreed with." She went on to critique the test, which she felt was not a true test of science skills or content. One of her students had struggled in particular with the difficult wording, and she commented, "So you are able to identify differences. However, you don't know what the word 'alternative' means. So to be able to analyze this and show a difference, you could do that easily – so that's the skill. But you are unable to read 'alternative' because you have some literacy issues. So it's not saying, you're not good at science, it's saying, you have trouble reading. So that test is not...showing comprehension, it's showing that they have difficulty with certain words."

As previously noted in this chapter, the science department at Washington required students to take assessments known as 'CRTs' at regular intervals throughout the year. The vignette, which describes the first such assessment June must give to her students, provides an example of June individuating—or an instance of a teacher-becoming—as an advocate for her students. Recognizing that several features of the assessment would create difficulties for her students, June went to the department chair and negotiated accommodations for the test that would help her students access the material and increase the chance that they would be successful (or indeed, make it more likely they would choose to participate in the assessment at all). However, this negotiation was possible because of multiple interacting factors—including June's own ideas about social justice and her previous positive interactions with her chair. Importantly, another first year teacher without these beliefs or with a different relationship with a department leader may not have been successful at such a negotiation or may not have undertaken it at all.

Although June was able to get permission to modify the size of the text and provide additional time for her students, she was still worried that they might react to the look of the test itself, including the complex language involved, by "shutting down," or becoming overwhelmed and refusing to participate. Rather than administering the test with these only two accommodations, June also decided to read items to her students and paraphrase the meaning if students were struggling to understand what the questions or items were asking them to do. In doing so, she hoped to "come into composition" with her students in a way that created an assemblage that enabled students to understand the content on the test and experience success, which she understood as critical to their continuing participation in her lessons on a daily basis. Throughout this vignette, we can observe multiple instances of June coming into composition with her students and interacting with them in ways that interrupted the ideal of the 'autonomous learner.' She worked them first as a whole class by explaining the purpose of the assessment and letting them know she believed in their ability to successfully complete the tasks on it: "All of you are capable of doing this." She also interacted with them individually, drawing on what she knew would work for them, such as telling Lydia, "You are too smart not to do this." When another student ran out of steam, June quietly read to her and prodded her to write the answer identified by the student.

This is also an example of the molecular work of the teacher that may potentially become a line of flight, or a break from the status quo. The assessment, and the order to administer it, is a molar force that would serve as a stoppage—to June's students, it would potentially shut them down for this class session, and perhaps even affect her students' future *becomings* in that class. However, the molecular lines, or the activity of June's classroom, must carry out the action of the molar line. If June had simply handed the tests out to her students and ordered them to complete it, observing the normalized expectations of testing (everyone works in isolation to demonstrate autonomous mastery), her molecular work would have reinforced the molar line and upheld the status quo for her special education students. That is, the students would have most likely failed the test through non-completion, which would have reinforced the label of special education as a student unable to meet "normal" educational expectations. Instead, their collective activity produced a momentary escape from the oppressive norm—June's students completed the assessment, and were successful doing so. At the end of the first semester, the data for each class's tests were collected, averaged, and compared across each class in the science department. June was ecstatic to report, "My students scored the highest out of every class." While the "scoring" reinforces another molar line—that of assigning a number value to students as a ranking system—it simultaneously demonstrates a disruption of the normal for special education students.

SUMMARY

June's case highlights the fascinating productions of interactions within an assemblage and the way those interactions provide the potential for unexpected developments, including lines of flight that disrupt the status quo and potentially produce larger changes in the system over time. Initially, June's new teaching position seemed to present *striated space* (Deleuze & Guattari, 1987) with many molar lines that would constrain her in enacting socially just, inquiry-based pedagogies. She was working in a school with a reputation for being challenging; was teaching special education without the preparation for it; and was working with students who had internalized the label of *disabled student* (Slater, 2012), thus making them more likely to resist participating in active learning opportunities. In such a context, June might have struggled to survive, as many first year teachers do (Chubbock et al., 2001; Feiman-Nemser, 1993; Veenman, 1984), returning to more traditional lecture-type methods to retain control of her classroom and mediate the demands of her new position (Allen, 2009; Cady, Meier, & Lubinski, 2006; Flores & Day, 2006). Yet, the ways that the different elements of June's assemblage fit together and functioned—her own qualities, her students, her small classes, her layers of support—produced becomings that were not predictable from initial conditions. That is, this unique mixture interacted to create new circumstances, which were often ones that often broke the expectations of what a first year teacher and what special education students can do, thus creating a smoother space within which to construct a socially just, inquiry-rich pedagogy.

Although June's context is admittedly unique, particularly because of her small class sizes, her experience with her students holds valuable insight for working with marginalized student populations who may resist more learner-centered experiences. By finding ways to respond to student needs, meeting them at their ability levels, and helping them bridge to required skills and competencies, June and her students co-constructed lines of flight that disrupted the molar category of "special needs student," the label given to a learner who is unsuccessful at "regular" or "mainstream" academic tasks (Goodley, 2007). Over time, her students built confidence as they experienced success and demonstrated scientific proficiencies. These lines of flight were constructed and reconstructed, resulting in increasing levels of student participation and learning in classroom activities.

USING RHIZOMATICS TO THINK DIFFERENTLY ABOUT TEACHING

INTRODUCTION

In this study, we investigated the teaching practices of three first-year science teachers, Mauro, Bruce, and June, who taught in the same urban, diverse, high-poverty district in the Northeastern United States. To study their teaching practices as complex, situated phenomena, we used concepts from rhizomatics (Deleuze & Guattari, 1987) to construct three case studies describing the practices that emerged over the fall semester of their school year. As we noted in our initial overview, rhizomatics appeals to us because it offers concepts that serve as analytic tools to think differently, and produce different ways of thinking (St. Pierre, 2004), about how teachers learn about teaching in preservice education and apply that learning in classrooms. Such thinking not only offers nuanced, contextually rich insights into the preparation and ongoing support of novice educators, but also disrupts dominant positivist, linear models of teacher learning, where teachers are positioned as isolated, autonomous actors who "do" teaching to students as a transaction. In contrast, we argue, teachers are part of assemblages that co-produce teaching through ongoing interactions, and as such, teaching (and the processes implicated therein) is fundamentally multiple, relational, and non-linear. In this chapter, we synthesize our analysis across the three cases presented, drawing on examples from the cases and concepts from rhizomatics to present different lines of thinking about the construction of first-year teaching practice.

TEACHING AS ASSEMBLAGE

One major shift implicated in rhizomatic thinking is moving from moving from the *one* to the *multiple*. For the present study, that means abandoning the humanistic view of teacher as an autonomous individual, and instead conceptualizing the teacher as part of a larger multiplicity. We argue that the concept of *assemblage* assists in this (re)conceptualization. An assemblage is both a noun and a verb. As a noun, an assemblage is a mixture of multiple elements (in this case, the teacher, students, context, and so on); as a verb, assemblage refers to the actual mixing of those elements, or how they work together. Each of us is a multiplicity—just so, the teacher is a constellation of previous experiences, ideas, intentions, and so forth. The teacher "plugs" herself into an assemblage comprised of classroom space, students, classroom routines, discourses of schooling, and so on (Defreitas, 2012), and the ways in which they come into composition enable different productions (teaching activity).

In each of the three cases discussed, a constellation of factors—including the initial preservice learning and beliefs the teachers brought with them, the ways they interacted with their students, and contextual elements—shaped and affected the practices teachers produced to different degrees and in different ways. For example, Mauro brought his own beliefs about social justice and his NUTR learning about problem posing, differentiation of learning, and building student relationships. Once he actually began teaching, his ability to enact practices consistent with these beliefs and understandings depended largely on the responses of his particular student populations and the ways he interacted with them. Because he was able to negotiate with his upperclassmen students in productive ways and was able to develop with them relationships, the teaching practices he constructed in his earth science classes were characterized by more equitable methods, such as open-ended questioning and experiential learning. He also began to develop a sense of teacher-self as a caring teacher with high expectations of his students. With his freshmen, however, he was not able to gain their cooperation for more open-ended activities, so he modified his teaching to include more direct instruction. The conflict Mauro experienced within these classes contributed to a more authoritarian enactment of teacher-self, or becoming-teacher.

Bruce, to a larger extent than Mauro, maintained some traditional beliefs about how his content area should be taught, which created conflict with his learning about inquiry from his preservice year with the NUTR. Although his students were generally cooperative with him, suggesting he did not have to negotiate directly with them for participation in most of the activities observed, contextual factors had a large influence on his practices. For instance, the drastic change in leadership that occurred two months into the school year and a lack of mentoring or administrative support contributed to Bruce's constant worries about his job performance. These external elements interacted with his internal pedagogical conflicts to produce practices that defied a consistent characterization. At times his teaching was transmission-based, and other times, learner-led and centered on student inquiry. These conflicts also produced contradictory teacher-selves. Within the classroom, Bruce was a caring, "zany" teacher who sought to provide creative learning opportunities for his students. In the larger school setting, however, Bruce felt compelled to follow his principal's more authoritarian mandates and "play it safe" so he could feel secure in keeping his job.

Finally, June began the year with a commitment to infusing her classes with questions and investigations. By continually modifying instruction to meet her individual students needs and successfully building relationships with them, she was able to enact practices that were inquiry-based and provided multiple entry points for class assignments and assessments so all her students could be academically successful. Her enactment of classroom practices was also supported by contextual factors, such as support provided by her department chair and colleagues, and the benefit of small classes. The interaction of these multiple elements helped shape her becoming-teacher as a caring, calm authority figure, a student advocate, and an emerging instructional leader.

One of the goals of this study was to investigate the ways that teachers' pre-professional learning moved across time and space into their first-year practices. In examining the first-year teacher-assemblages presented here, we suggest that each teacher's learning was only one component in the multiplicity of the teacher her/himself. That multiplicity, in turn, is only one part of the first-year assemblage, which includes any number of elements, as noted above: the teacher herself (and her multiplicity), the students (and all the elements they bring), the components and physical space of the classroom, the larger school context, and so on. Further, the teacher's learning, as it comes into composition with new populations of students, contextual elements, and ongoing interactions, continues to morph.

Importantly, preservice learning itself is not monolithic, but rather has many moving parts. A pedagogical vision itself is a multiplicity, and as the first-year teachers learned about the key ideas and practices in their pre-service program, these were collaboratively negotiated among the constellation of elements present in the residency—with the faculty, other teacher candidates in the program, the teachers' own beliefs and backgrounds, and the school context in which they were working. Upon moving into the first year of teaching, each teacher enacted practices that were products of multiple, ongoing negotiations with their learning, themselves, their students, and their context. In this way, we argue that the ideas from the teachers' preservice learning were not transferred whole, nor were they a pure "application" of knowledge (Korthgen & Kessels, 1999) from the NUTR program. Instead, they were *translated*. That is, although there were some common elements that might be attributed to their preservice learning, the different mixtures of teacher-students-context produced hybrids that were substantially different. Each of the three teachers' practices, for example, had some elements of inquiry-based instruction, but they appeared differently because of the unique ways the teacher-assemblages fit together and operated. For example, in his earth science classes, Mauro relied on problem-posing through teacher-led activities and demonstrations. Bruce vacillated between tightly structured teacher-led instruction and completely unstructured student inquiry projects. June, as a third illustration, considered inquiry the foundation of her teaching, but worked intensely to provide student scaffolds and guided them step-by-step much of the time.

From examining these three cases and the ways the teaching practices were constructed, it is clear that no straight line exists between what these teachers learned in their preservice program and the practices they enacted in their first year of teaching. Indeed, no one-to-one causal relations may be drawn from an analysis of a teaching assemblage—instead, Deleuze suggests that there are only "quasi-causes" that contribute to what is produced by different mixtures (Deleuze, 1990). That is, the elements that are present in particular assemblages interact with each other and collectively contribute to an outcome. Even if those elements are isolated, however, none of them can be the cause—only a contributor, or a quasi-cause, along with the rest of the assemblage. In such an analysis, the relationships between elements become even more important than the elements themselves, which is a point we take up next.

THE RELATIONAL AND INTER-RELATIONAL WORK OF TEACHING

We suggest that investigating the way elements in an assemblage work together—or the process of "coming into composition"—is a productive analytic site when pursuing inquiry from a rhizomatic frame. As Deleuze and Guattari (1987) note, "Any point on a rhizome can be connected to anything other, and must be" (p. 7). The work of the rhizome occurs via these "ceaselessly establish[ed] connections" (p. 7)—as does any kind of social activity, including that which occurs in the classroom. In addition, as more and more connections are made, the nature of multiplicities change. In other words, as elements, bodies, and discourses collide in a particular space, there is an encounter that changes the multiplicity as a whole and affects what is produced. Understood in the context of this study, the objects, ideas, people, and spaces with which the teacher connects—her students, the school culture, other teachers, school leadership, resources available, and so on—irrevocably shape the teaching activity that is produced. Thus, the work of the teacher is always relational, or tied to multiple actors, forces, and materials present in her setting. Further, this work is also *inter-relational*, indicating there is multidirectional action occurring that is simultaneously shaping the practices that are emerging. In this way, we argue that the work of the teacher is actually co-constituted by multiple factors and influences, which vary by the nature of the teaching-assemblage. All three cases demonstrate these relational and interrelational processes of jointly produced teaching practices. Below, we discuss two major factors besides the teachers themselves in the co-production of the practices—student interactions and contextual conditions—and examine the relations therein.

Interacting with Students

In all three cases, the way teachers connected to and interacted with students surfaced as an important influence in the construction of practice (although to different degrees for each teacher). Indeed, the very type of teaching they were seeking to enact—learner centered, inquiry-based, culturally and linguistically responsive instruction—is predicated on student participation as given. In other words, to be successful, this type of teaching requires learners to actively take part in a lesson in specific ways. When considered from this perspective, then, students are important co-producers of the practices that new teachers are able to enact, and thus the interactions teachers have with students must foster an environment where students are inclined to do so. As some researchers have argued, and this study also suggests, building relationships with students, particularly marginalized populations, is key to securing their active participation in classroom activities (e.g., Delpit, 1995; Villegas & Lucas, 2002).

Mauro's case, because of the differences between the relationships he was able to forge with his two sets of students, serves as a particularly strong example of how teacher-student relationships might shape teaching practices. Although Mauro initially used the same strategies for relationship-building in both classes, his upper-classmen seemed to appreciate his efforts toward transparency and attempts to get to know them through in-class "side-conversations." His ninth graders, however, did not receive these strategies positively, and he was not able to develop the same rapport with them that he had with his earth science students. Instead, he felt forced to resort to more transmission-based teaching methods and classroom management techniques, which he disliked. This development, in turn, caused him internal tension. Thus, despite some surface similarities in context and the use of the same relationship building techniques, the different elements of Mauro's assemblages and the ways they came together and interacted produced different practices.

June's account not only supports the importance of teacher-student relationships in enacting learner-centered practices, but also highlights the empowering possibilities that can emerge from them. June's students were both urban students of color and were classified as special needs students, meaning that she may have encountered particularly heavy resistance from them to participating in her inquiry-based lessons. As adolescents of color likely disconnected from the white norms of formal schooling (Ogbu, 1982), and as students who had been separated out from the general population and labeled as cognitively inferior (Slater, 2012; Allan, 2011), they were unlikely either to see value in actively participating, nor have the confidence to do so. Yet June was successful a good deal of the time in engaging her students through a variety of strategies and providing intensive supports. A critical piece that seemed to contribute to both relationship development and the building of student confidence was June's proleptic view of her students—meaning that she constantly treated her students as if they had scientific skills they had not yet mastered. By consistently demonstrating that she believed they were capable, while simultaneously providing them with the supports and encouragement needed to successfully engage in increasingly cognitively complex tasks, June "came into composition" with her students in ways that moved beyond ensuring her students' participation in her activities and actually disrupted, within her class, the normalized category of "special education student."

All three cases also demonstrate the importance of attending to the *inter-relational* aspects of the teaching assemblage. For each of Mauro, June, and Bruce, some contextual elements came into composition differently in their assemblages, thereby producing developments that diverged from what initial conditions might have suggested would occur. For instance, Mauro taught in the same school in which he spent his pre-professional practical experience, which some studies have shown to be a supportive factor (e.g, Hebert & Worthy 2001; Lambson, 2010). Yet, beginning his first year in a school where he was familiar with the context, his colleagues, and the population of students did not automatically assure him success. At least one of Mauro's classes presented extreme behavioral challenges for him and contributed to the adoption of teacher-centered instruction and an authoritarian classroom persona.

June, in contrast, accepted a position that seemed like it might present difficulties on several levels. The school had a reputation for having the city's most challenging students, the context differed from her pre-service placement in an arts-themed magnet school, and she was to teach special education biology, although she had no explicit preparation to teach in a special needs setting. Despite these daunting circumstances, however, June was able to experience much more success with her students than seemed possible, given the challenges she faced. Instead, a few unexpected elements of her setting—such as the support provided by her department chair and very small classes—became enabling factors. Together with the relationships she was able to build with students and her own personal qualities, all these elements worked together to support the enactment of equity-minded pedagogy.

Bruce and his students provide yet a third illustration of the unpredictability of interactions in an assemblage. Given his pre-service professors' concern about his ability to relate to students, his easy relationships with his students were a surprising development— albeit one that could be explained by the obvious efforts he put into showing his trust and care for them, combined with the enthusiasm and natural curiosity the students seemed to bring. From these conditions, students were usually eager to participate in his lessons. This circumstance may have provided a measure of support for him and contributed to his efforts to hold on to some of the elements of his preservice learning, such as occasional projects or student-led problem solving. If this element had changed—that is, if he had been faced with the difficulties existing within the school as well as had challenging or uncooperative students—he may have abandoned his attempts to teach in equitable ways.

Negotiating with Context

In addition to students, contextual factors in the setting and the ways in which each teacher interacted with them had some influence on the teaching practices that were produced. The notion that "context matters" in teaching is a finding corroborated by many studies of first year practice (e.g., Allebone, 2006; Bianchini & Cazavos, 2007; Chubbock et al., 2001; Fry, 2007; Scherff, 2008). Yet, we argue that, from a rhizomatic perspective, an analysis of the contextual negotiations also highlights the role of the material, non-human elements of teaching assemblages. An important shift in rhizomatics is from the Enlightenment human-centered paradigm to one in which there are no divisions between subject and object, between mind and body, or between human and non-human. With this lens, we can appreciate that the material world and even the non-tangible, such as ideas, have the capacity to affect, and can shape teaching practices just as much—and in some cases more—than human actors.

In Bruce's case, both human and non-human contextual factors in his setting profoundly influenced his teaching in the classroom. Bruce began the year in an environment with factors known to hinder new teachers in their enactment of particular types of pedagogy—such as a lack of resources (Castro, Kelly, & Shih, 2010; Starkey, 2010; Tait, 2008), a mandated curriculum (Brashier & Norris, 2008; Ferguson-Patrick, 2011), a dysfunctional school organization (Scherff, 2008) and a lack of consistent and appropriate mentorship (Hargreaves & Jacka, 1995; Hebert & Worthy, 2001; Stanulis, Fallona, & Pearson, 2002). In addition to these already constraining circumstances, three months into the school year, there was a leadership change. The new principal was focused on discipline, valued a more traditional conception of teaching, and was considering eliminating Bruce's position for the next year. The inter-relational effect of these conditions, in combination with Bruce's own internal struggle between more traditional forms of teaching and the type of equitable pedagogy he had learned in his preservice program, produced erratic practices veering between more directive, teacher-centered instruction and collaborative problem-solving or inquiry-driven projects.

Mauro and June also were influenced by their contextual elements, although to a slightly lesser degree than Bruce. Mauro, for instance, felt more pressure to cover certain content in his environmental classes because they were tested, another environmental circumstance that tends to challenge new teachers (Bergeron, 2008; Saka, Southerland, & Brooks, 2009). His earth science classes, in contrast, were not subject to standardized assessments, and without this constraint, Mauro was more likely to take a flexible approach to his lessons. Feeling less pressure to meet a particular set of curricular criteria in a set amount of time, in combination with his earth science students' cooperation, influenced his willingness to pursue side conversations with students as they made spontaneous connections between content and their own experiences and knowledge. In turn, these "side conversations" became an important factor in the building of relationships with these particular sets of students.

TEACHER IDENTITY AND BECOMING

As mentioned in the beginning of this chapter, taking up the more relational view of teaching articulated above and the use of the more connected construct of "assemblage" moves us away from viewing the teacher as encapsulated individual and toward conceptualizing the teacher *as* a multiplicity (a dynamic network of beliefs, experiences, personal qualities) *within* a multiplicity (as a part of a larger system of forces, bodies, discourses, and so on). This shift also carries implications for the construct of teacher identity, since it problematizes the idea that teachers can develop a stable teacher-self. As other researchers (e.g., Olsen, 2008; Beijard, Meijer, & Verloop, 2004) have argued, teacher identity is not one thing, but rather an ongoing, dynamic, constantly evolving process both shaped by the self and the context in which the self is implicated. Perhaps then, the construct of teacher identity itself, the label of which indicates sameness (Roy, 2003), is an inappropriate to describe and analyze what is actually an ongoing process of change.

In each of the cases, the teachers not only developed and enacted multiple teacher selves, but *became-different* in relation to the various constellation of factors and forces occurring inside and outside their classrooms at any given time. As we have suggested throughout the chapters in this book, the notion of *becoming* can help provide an alternative view of teacher development. *Becoming,* which is both a noun and a verb expressing change, offers a way to discuss teacher development in a way that does not implicate linearity, consistency, and/or directionality, as stage-based theories have in the past (e.g., Fuller, 1969; Berliner, 1988). Rather, analyzing teacher developments as *becomings* allows for both a more textured view of multiple, seemingly contradictory identity enactments, as well as insight into the processes of becoming-different over time.

Returning to the example of Bruce, the lens of becoming provides for an understanding of his identity development as *event* (Deleuze, 1990). That is, we theorize that no identity existed for him outside of a particular situation. Rather, what the literature commonly refers to as "teacher identity" was actually an enactment of a momentary, co-constructed self in response to a set of particular circumstances. Put a different way, this was an "individuation"—a temporarily realized teacher-individual. Thus, in the classroom, Bruce might have individuated as a creative and caring person with his students on days when a particular constellation of elements coalesced – perhaps he might be feeling less pressure from his principal, the class was not interrupted, and he had planned a conceptually-driven lesson to which students responded enthusiastically. On other days, when a different set of circumstances arose—maybe when multiple interruptions occurred in his class, he was focusing on more mathematical and procedural elements that students found less interesting, or the notion of job security was weighing particularly heavy on him—he might appear as a more traditional, transmission-focused teacher. Thus, each of these examples of identity-enactment might be seen as instances of *becoming.*

CONSTRUCTING A PEDAGOGY OF EQUITY IN URBAN SCHOOLS

A third line of thinking flowing from this study concerns the construction of teaching practices that interrupt institutional norms of instruction and schooling, and thus, pursue goals of equity in education and society at large (Cochran Smith et al., 2009). Examining the interaction of elements within the teaching assemblages of Mauro, June, and Bruce as they attempted to enact the type of equitable practices learned in their preservice teacher preparation programs may help to inform thinking about what Zeichner (2010a) dubs a "perennial problem" of teacher education—the difficulty of enacting particular theories in practice. The majority of teacher preparation programs now teach pedagogy aligned with social constructivist views of learning, and many also focus on pedagogy that meets the needs of culturally and linguistically diverse learners (Cochran Smith & Villegas, 2016). Yet, even with this preparation, and despite a wealth of conceptual and empirical research condemning it, the banking method (Freire, 1970) of transmission teaching and autocratic classroom dynamics still remain the dominant pattern in schools, especially those located in highly diverse, high-poverty urban areas (Achinstein, Ogawa, & Seiglman, 2005; Haberman, 1995/2010; Solomon, Singer, Campbell, & Allan, 2011). Why?

As we argued earlier in this chapter, translating pedagogical principles learned in initial teacher preparation into classroom practice is a complex, multi-faceted process involving multiple actors, setting elements, and ideas, occurring by way of connection and interaction to produce teaching practices. However, when specifically discussing the translation of pedagogy grounded in principles of social justice, yet another layer of complexity must be addressed. The type of equitable pedagogy we outlined in chapter two, and that our three participants were attempting to put into practice, breaks from the ingrained teaching methods of the status quo. In other words, enacting teaching methods advancing goals of equity means battling the dominant power structures that exist both in society and schools, which are microcosms of the larger social system (Bourdieu, 1973).

We suggest that a rhizomatic analysis of the molar, molecular, and lines of flight may illuminate the additional layer of complexity of attempting to teach for social justice as a beginning teacher. Molar lines, or dominant power structures and discourses, are rigid forces that bind social activity to the status quo (Deleuze & Guattari, 1987). Molar lines include external institutional structures that reinforce the standard norms in schools (Albrecht-Crane & Slack, 2003), such as the bell schedules, mandated testing, curricular standards, and/or bureaucratic dysfunction. In addition, molar lines encompass ideas and beliefs that may be internalized by teachers and students (Strom & Martin, 2013).

However, molar lines must be translated into day-to-day action by molecular lines. Molar lines are just the rigid "overcoding"—the actual work must be carried out by supple, molecular lines, which comprise micropolitics. Because these lines are flexible, they might enact the normalizing work of dominant power structures and discourses, but they also have the potential to break from the status quo and become "lines of flight" (Deleuze & Guattari, 1987). As suggested previously, the work of the teacher is *molecular*. Her work is stratified by many molar lines, which might be internal to the teacher herself, present in her classroom, and/or imposed from the school, district, and state/federal policy mandates. Yet, she and her students, and a range of other material and incorporeal elements, must actually carry out the day-to-day actions that enforce these molar structures—and they do have some agency to resist them as well. In classrooms, possibilities always exist for momentary escape, a break from the status quo of instruction. These escapes might take the form of a conversation in class that fuses academic and personal elements, like one of Mauro's side conversations, a moment of student-teacher connection that transcends traditional power roles, or a student's surprised and excited shout in reaction to a demonstration of scientific phenomena. These escapes are temporal—the class session must end for the day, eventually the conversation must come back around to the objective of the activity or lesson, or the teacher once again must assume the role of the class authority. Yet, those momentary lines of flight do produce changes, although perhaps they may not immediately be noticeable. However, in returning to the molar norms of practice, a shift or mutation occurs in the overall system. Although it may be perhaps too small to produce any discernable change at the actual moment the line of flight occurs, if constructed and re-constructed over time, this infinitesimal shuffling of molar lines produces changes on a greater scale. These larger changes might be realized as eventual transformations over time, which lead, for example, to the gathering of a critical mass or tipping point leading to social movements or other systemic transformations. As Deleuze and Guattari (1987) explain, "The profound movements stirring a society present themselves in this fashion…from the viewpoint of micropolitics, a society is defined by its lines of flight" (p. 216). Drawing on these concepts, we argue that rhizomatics provides a theory of social change that might be applied at the level of the classroom to help us understand both the terrain of teaching in urban schools for new teachers and the process(es) of enacting practices grounded in principles of equity and social justice.

From an analysis of the rhizomatic lines constituting the movements of the teaching-assemblages we studied, we suggest that all three teachers worked in spaces that were stratified, or comprised of many molar lines. Yet the ways the teachers perceived their contexts and worked together with other elements within their settings—that is, the molecular lines they co-constructed within their multiplicities—shaped what they were able to do pedagogically. Mauro, for example, taught two different science content areas, both of which were "low-track" (in this case, these were science classes intended for students who had been identified as low performing in mathematics and thus deemed as unlikely to successfully complete physics or chemistry). His ninth-grade assemblages were characterized by both difficult contextual circumstances (such as being a tested subject, large classes, and Mauro's own newness to the subject) and challenging student interactions, which contributed to a normalization of Mauro's practice to teacher-led instruction and autocratic classroom management. Thus, Mauro's molecular work with his ninth grade class largely reinforced the work of molar lines. Yet, while this description mainly characterizes Mauro's instruction and classroom interactions during the observations conducted in his ninth grade classes over his first few months of teaching, lines of flight, or moments of disruption from the status quo, were also visible occasionally. While these did not materialize into larger changes while this study was being conducted, Mauro and his students' co-construction of practice is ongoing, and transformations might have been evident across a longer time span.

In contrast, Mauro's earth science classes presented elements that, when interacting with his attempts to enact his preservice learning and negotiation strategies, created a "smoother space" (Deleuze & Guattari, 1987) for constructing a pedagogy that broke from the status quo of more traditional, transmission based teaching in urban schools. In Mauro's day-to-day activities with his earth science students, multiple lines of flight were evident in our observations. By focusing on problem-posing and experiential learning, Mauro's classes were replete with questions and opportunities for students to think about scientific phenomena and actively co-construct knowledge (rather than merely receiving it). This type of pedagogy represents a break not only from the traditional model of teaching as a uni-directional transmission of information from teacher to student, but also interrupts the positivist conception of knowledge as information that comes from "without," or is already existing out there, moderated by experts (Dewey, 1938, p. 17). Instead, Mauro's students were invited to engage with their own previous knowledge, the earth science content, facilitated learning experiences, and each other, to create contextual understanding. This activity, then, positioned them as knowers and thinkers, which ruptured the molar category of "students of low-track science" and the "cognitively deficient" implication with which this classification comes (Oakes, 1985/2005).

Alongside these instructional lines of flight, Mauro and his upperclassmen students' co-construction of an open, easy social environment enabled collective engagement in tangential side conversations, forging connections between teacher and students. These connections momentarily blurred the student/teacher binary, transforming them into student-teachers and teacher-students (Freire, 1970). That is, they temporarily broke out of the molar categories of "student" and "teacher" into a "third space outside the binary of teacher and student that yet allows for the subjectivity of both" (Shapiro, 2009, p. 423). These ruptures opened up spaces where different and more fluid ways of thinking, being, teaching, and learning were possible. Reconstructed over time, these lines of flight in Mauro's earth science classes contributed to his ability to enact practices that were more learner-centered, meaningful, and relevant for his students.

An analysis of the molar and molecular activity of Bruce's case illuminates the conflict that can develop from attempting to translate equitable pedagogies into practice when intensely constrained by both internal and external molar lines (and the ways they cross over into each other). Bruce's teaching was not just "overcoded" by difficult contextual elements—such as the dysfunction of the school, the lack of resources and consistent instructional support, and tumultuous school leadership change—but was simultaneously constrained by normalizing or disciplinary forces he himself had internalized. These internalized discourses manifested in Bruce's traditional beliefs about teaching and his performance-related fears of straying too far from the norm of instruction. The combination and interaction of these multiple molar lines at the institutional level and individual level contributed to the construction of practices that echoed traditional approaches to instruction. Bruce tended to separate conceptual and mathematic physics elements, and often presented ideas to students through lecture or other forms of teacher-led, whole-class instruction.

Yet, despite the rigid circumstances he faced from the challenging combination of imposed and internalized molar lines, Bruce did not abandon his preservice teaching entirely in favor of transmission-based, authoritarian teaching practices, as many novice teachers tend to do (Allan, 2009; Saka, Southerland, & Brooks, 2009; Veenman, 1984; Zeichner & Tabachnik, 1981). His lessons did, at times, contain some evidence of experiential learning in the form of "break-out demonstrations" of physics phenomena, collaborative student-led problem solving, and inquiry-based labs. The appearance of these activities, albeit inconsistently, provides evidence of the supple, molecular lines present at the level of the classroom that characterize the day-to-day activity of the teacher and her students. Although in Bruce's case, much of the molecular activity occurring in his classroom did approximate traditional instructional norms, lines of flight also broke away and enabled some elements of equitable teaching, such as the cultivation of relationships with his students, particularly ones labeled by the school as "difficult" or "challenging."

As a third example of molar and molecular analysis, June's account provides a particularly hopeful example of the potential for equitable teaching even when facing seemingly extraordinary stratification. Despite the previously noted molar lines within her setting that seemed likely to constrain her teaching, the multiple levels of support available, her own personal qualities, and small classes were contextual conditions that together created a smooth(er) space (Deleuze & Guattari, 1987) in which to enact inquiry-based teaching practices. Within this space, June and her students produced lines of flight that disrupted the label of "special needs student," and instead experienced moments of, for example, becoming-scientist. This assemblage also, at least in the temporal space of June's classroom, disturbed the molar norm of the ideal learner in a neoliberal society (typically a student who can demonstrate mastery of content autonomously). Goodley (2007) explains how this norm is bound up with current political ideals, arguing that the autonomous learner "mimics the kind of individualistic personhood valued by the neoliberal, marketized society" (p. 320). June and her students, instead, *came into composition*, forming a rhizome that provided both collaborative support and multiple entry points so that collectively, students could accomplish tasks of which they had been previously deemed incapable. As her students experienced success and gained confidence, they became more willing to participate actively in her lessons and attempt high-level learning tasks, which we argue points to evidence of larger changes in the local, stratified system of June's school.

Through our analysis, we have suggested that the creation of an equitable pedagogy, particularly for first-year teachers in urban school settings, may be viewed as lines of flight (re)constructed over time to produce larger and more sustained transformations within a school system. Importantly, however, because the work of the teacher occurs in a rigid social space tightly bound with normalizing structures, and is co-constituted by interactions with so many other elements of her assemblage(s), lines of flight occur unpredictably, in fits and starts. Thus, (co)constructing a pedagogy of equity and social justice will not be smooth. Given the ubiquitousness of the molar lines that they must navigate, particularly in our current climate of market-driven accountability reform, we should not expect that new teachers will be able to seamlessly plan and facilitate learner-centered, inquiry-based activities when they initially enter their classrooms. Over time, however, if the teacher can work together with her students and contextual conditions in productive ways, the activity of the assemblage may produce lines of flight. If enough breaks from the status quo of instruction and other components of the "grammar of schooling" (Tyack & Tobin, 1994) occur, these may add up to larger changes within the system.

PUTTING RHIZOMATICS TO WORK

Informing Practice, Policy, & Research

INTRODUCTION

As we have argued throughout this book, thinking about teaching with rhizomatics disrupts current neoliberal conceptualizations of educational activity in favor of a fluid, multiplistic, non-linear perspective—and as such entails multiple shifts (Ovens, Strom, & Garbett, 2016), which are detailed in the chart below. The more prevalent and dominant positivist conceptions define teaching as an individual act with causal correspondence (something the teacher does as she transfers her learning from her preservice preparation into the classroom), takes a static view of development (she is effective or is not), reduces teaching to quantifiable indicators (such as scores on rubrics or value-added measurements), focuses on questions of substance and/ or product (*Is this teacher effective? What are students' achievement outcomes?*), and expects teachers to reproduce the same kinds of practices taught to them in their teacher preparation programs.

Table 1. Rhizomatic Shifts in Thinking

From the autonomous individual	to the interactive multiplicity
From causal linearity	to heterogenous connectivity
From reduction	to proliferation and complexity
From static being	to fluid becoming
From a focus on substance/products	to process and function
From sameness	to difference

From a rhizomatic view, teaching phenomena emerges from a multiplicity of which the individual is just one element, and that production of teaching emerges as a function of the mixture of heterogenous connections being made (also known as the *quasi-cause* of teaching) (Deleuze, 1990). By focusing on constellations of elements and their collective activity, the proliferation of connections may be explored and complexity is embraced as essential. Further, in this perspective, *being* gives way to the more fluid *becoming*, a radically different, non-normative ontology corresponding to a dynamic, constantly changing reality. Acknowledging that we, and the world around us, are in a perpetual state of flux, it is impossible for teachers working with different populations of students, in different settings with different contextual conditions, to produce the same types of practices. Hence, rhizomatics stresses the production of *difference*. The focus of inquiry, too, shifts to questions of process (how does it work?) and context (how does it work *for you*?).

In this final chapter, we offer implications for teaching, teacher education, and related research and policy, in light of these rhizomatic shifts. We begin by discussing teacher preparation, describing ways that teacher educators and teacher education programs can help future teachers engage with the complexity they will encounter in their future classrooms. We then suggest ways that school leaders can better support new teachers as they work to translate their pre-professional learning during their first year of practice and beyond. Finally, we offer policy and research implications that account for teaching as non-linear, multiplistic activity.

PUTTING RHIZOMATICS TO WORK IN TEACHER EDUCATION

The cases presented in this book provide evidence that no one-to-one, causal correspondence may be drawn between initial teacher preparation and the practices that are eventually enacted in teachers' classrooms. The learning teachers do in their pre-service programs becomes only one element influencing the teacher, along with factors like personal beliefs and her own experiences as a student. As she enters the classroom, the teacher (and her multiplicity) is only one element in the larger teaching assemblage (her students, the context, and so on) that influences the eventual practices that are constructed. We suggest, however, that preservice preparation has the potential to be a more powerful influence in shaping the work of future teacher-assemblages. Specifically, by adopting a more ecological model of coursework and field experience, as well as attending to the relational aspect of enacting teaching practice, teacher preparation can more strategically support future teachers in translating equitable teaching methods into their first-year settings.

Ecological Models of Teacher Preparation

Typical models of university-based teacher preparation feature a set of courses taken on campus that provide students with requisite theoretical understandings, followed by a clinical practicum at a school site. In contrast, Mauro, Bruce, and June attended a "hybrid" teacher preparation program that was taught in an integrated, ecological format (Klein et al., 2013) that involved spending an entire academic year in a clinical apprenticeship in an urban high school, during which they received dual mentoring from a collaborative teacher and program faculty. Although we do not suggest that this ecological teacher education model may be directly linked in a causal manner to the eventual practices that emerged in the three teachers' classrooms, some evidence of benefit is visible. For example, in her first interview, June credited her preservice internship as providing her with practice for creating and supporting students in inquiry-based units. Working with urban students for an entire year also provided experience building the relationships that would be critical to her and her students' successes. Mauro's experiences planning earth science curriculum during his year of clinical practice contributed to his being asked to lead the earth science curriculum mapping and collaborative planning. Mauro also referenced the importance of learning to differentiate his lessons and teach via small group instruction, which he gained from his collaborating teacher, in helping him to meet the needs of his classes (although these methods appeared in his earth science classes more often than in his environmental science classes).

Bruce, however, seemed to have a more complicated relationship with his preservice learning. While circumstances in his context may have contributed to a partial "washing out" of the type of practices learned in his preservice education (Zeichner & Tabachnik, 1981), Bruce still clung to some elements of his pedagogical preparation from the NUTR—suggesting the possibility of belief change, or at least partial change, of even his most rigid and deep-set beliefs about instruction. Bruce refused to abandon his conviction that quality teaching was inquiry-based and learner-centered, even when confronted with the possibility of losing his job. As he stated in his last interview, "If [the principal] wants me to be completely traditional, maybe this isn't the best place for me."

The experiences of Mauro, Bruce, and June, to varying degrees, support educational scholars' and teacher educators' calls to more closely tie initial teacher preparation coursework and clinical practice in schools (e.g., Zeichner, 2010; Feiman-Nemser, 2001) and to increase the intensity and length of preservice fieldwork experiences (Darling-Hammond & Bransford, 2005). Sustained opportunities to engage in recursive cycles of collective meaning-making between teachers, students, and their context, where students of teaching can practice the contextual negotiation that occurs in classrooms, are critical. The facility to plan and productively enact inquiry-based lessons while simultaneously working together with a host of potential student and contextual factors takes time to develop, as Britzman (1991) notes in the title of her study, "Practice makes practice." Although the three teachers featured in this study were by no means "finished" when they entered the classroom—that is, their development and learning were and are ongoing—a year-long, integrated, contextualized, and supported apprenticeship experience seemed to contribute to the translation of at least some of the components of their preservice preparation into their first-year practices, even in the most constraining of environments, such as the one Bruce faced.

Research on preservice preparation highlights how some universities are working to more directly connect teacher learning in university coursework to field experiences in schools (Villegas & Cochran-Smith, 2016) as well as increase the actual amount of time teaching candidates spend in clinical practice before entering the classroom as the teacher of record (Bullough, Draper, & Young, 2004). Such reforms take the field a step closer to an apprenticeship model. Yet many teacher education programs retain the traditional separation of preparation into two separate stages, one involving coursework and one encompassing a field-based practicum

(Grossman, Hammerness, & McDonald, 2009). Because of a variety of factors, such as the operation of the university and school as separate entities, the lack of communication and collaboration between them, and their pursuit of disparate agendas (Valencia, Martin, Place, & Grossman, 2009), student teachers' experiences are rarely consistent with their coursework (Zeichner, 2010a). This major disconnect perpetuates what researchers have termed the theory/practice divide (Feiman-Nemser & Buchmann, 1985; Grossman, Hammerness, & McDonald, 2009) and ultimately reinforces the status quo of teaching.

While the disconnect between the milieus and agendas of universities and schools is evident, the *theory/practice divide* sets up a false binary between theory on the one hand and practice on the other. This term indicates that "theory" is housed in the university with faculty, and "practice" occurs in schools, which reifies problematic and historical power imbalances between these two settings. However, theory and practice are not discrete entities that are the purview of either universities or schools. They are entangled, interconnected, recursively informing each other, each already implicated in the other—or as Taguchi (2007) puts it, "We are *already* speaking and performing theory into this (messy) existence of practice" (p. 278). Researchers who use the language of "theory/practice divide" would likely agree that the methods that are most commonly observed in classrooms, such as lecture-based teaching and authoritarian classroom management, do have theories that explain them—such as behaviorist views of learning (Skinner, 1976), positivist views of knowledge as coming from "without" (Dewey, 1938), and understandings of the teacher's role as keeping students docile and obedient (Foucault, 1976). The term *theory-practice divide,* then, really does not denote a chasm that exists between two separate entities, since practice is never absent of theory—instead it indicates that teacher graduates are enacting practices informed by theories that are different than the ones teacher preparation programs tend to teach and promote.

Given the entangled nature of theory and practice, as well as the notion that future teachers bring deep-seated beliefs about how to teach (Lortie, 1975; Pajares, 1992; Richardson, 1997), programs of teacher education that closely integrate coursework and fieldwork may provide opportunities to surface and problematize the implicit theories implicated in the beliefs students of teaching tend to bring (and that inform more traditional teaching models, as noted above). In this process, teacher educators can avoid viewing teacher candidates as blank slates to be "filled" with the correct knowledge, and instead help them gain awareness of the beliefs and unarticulated theories they possess, and engage them in interrogating those vis-à-vis contemporary theories of teaching and learning (Taguchi, 2007). With closely-tied opportunities to engage in this learning through field experiences, future teachers can extend this problematizing to enacting instruction in the classroom. One way this work might materialize is through recursive inquiry cycles in which teacher candidates co-construct new understandings about learning theory with classmates and their instructor(s), enact that learning in a practice setting, and return to their class(es) to discuss, reflect, and problematize their classroom experiences as well as their own learning about theory-practice (Taylor, Klein, Onore, Strom, & Abrams, 2016).

Such recursive cycles of theorizing, practicing, and reflecting offer teachers opportunities to examine and problematize the complexity of applying their learning about pedagogy into situated practice—which may help to address the reality shock or "praxis shock" that new teachers tend to experience when challenged to enact the utopian vision of pedagogy they frequently develop in their preservice programs (Chubbock, 2008; Rushton, 2001; Smagorinsky, Gibson, Bickmore, Moore, & Cook, 2004; Veenman, 1984). In many university-based teacher preparation programs, the disconnect previously mentioned between coursework and practice means that students of teaching learn about pedagogy in a setting devoid of specific context and are presented an ideal version of teaching methods (Korthagen, Loughran, & Russell, 2006). As they begin their first year of teaching, however, novice educators face the herculean task of moving decontextualized and idealized teaching methods into settings with varied contextual conditions that they must navigate, with specific populations of students who may or may not respond to the teacher's instruction as anticipated. Such activity takes place in a system with rigid structures that routinely fail to enable the types of pedagogy generally promoted in today's teacher education programs, and within the larger neoliberal policy landscape stressing standards and accountability.

The major pedagogical work of new teachers, then, is to negotiate their preservice learning with all the actors, elements, and conditions in their new settings (that is, to *translate* it into context). We argue that to prepare future teachers to tackle this work, teacher educators have the responsibility to ensure that they are not just presenting idealized notions of pedagogy, but also providing the opportunity for students of teaching to trouble that utopian vision in light of factors that will mediate it (and will affect their own ability to agentically enact it). As mentioned above, in programs that tightly connect or integrate coursework and fieldwork, students of teaching might focus on inquiring into, reflecting upon, and collaboratively discussing problems encountered as they attempt to move their learning into action. In programs that offer separate or more disconnected coursework and practical experiences, however, future teachers can still problematize the concepts and theories they are learning through the use of richly descriptive case studies of teaching practice and videos of actual teaching.

As previously noted, some teacher preparation programs are increasing the time spent in practice and rethinking how to more closely connect coursework to field experiences. At the same time, the dramatic expansion of alternate route teacher certification programs (Darling-Hammond, 1990, 2009; Zeichner, 2010b) presents an obstacle to these efforts. Created to address teacher shortages in high-needs areas, alternate route programs place individuals with little or no professional preparation into classrooms (Baines, 2010; Darling-Hammond, 2006). Teachers entering the classroom though alternate routes normally must complete teacher preparation coursework within the first few years to receive a full teacher certification (Chin, Young, & Floyd, 2004), but the quality of this preparation varies widely (Darling-Hammond, 1990; Humphrey & Wechsler, 2007). This means, then, that when alternately certified teachers enter the classroom, they bring little or no preservice learning with which to negotiate their classroom experiences. Thus, from a rhizomatic perspective, the component of pedagogical knowledge—which was shown to be a mediating factor of teaching practice in all three of the cases presented in this study—is not even present in the teacher multiplicity, or teacher system, to influence the teaching practices constructed by alternate route teachers. Without the benefit of pre-professional learning and experiences, the central influence shaping instructional practice from the teacher herself is likely to be her own background experiences, world view, and beliefs about teaching stemming from her own time as a student in K-12 classrooms—which tend to reinforce transmission-based teaching patterns (Lortie, 1975; Pajares, 1992). This is even more concerning given that the majority of alternatively-certified teachers are placed in high-poverty schools (Darling-Hammond, 2010) and thus are at risk of perpetrating the status quo for our most vulnerable students.

Attending to the Relational Aspects of Teaching Practice

The cases described in this book support the notion that teaching does not happen in isolation, as the controlled action of a single (teacher) actor. Rather, it is a relational, highly interactive process (Britzman, 1991; Bullough, 1997; Bullough, Draper, & Young, 2004) involving a constellation of human actors, discourses, contextual elements, and so on. This multiplistic conception of teaching conflicts with the commonsense Western logic that serves as the foundation of our collective neoliberal mindset, which stresses the agency of the individual (St. Pierre, 2004). Neoliberal common sense, which in its current form stems from the rationalism of the Enlightenment (Giroux, 2002), suggests individuals are thinking subjects who define existence by that well-known Cartesian statement: "I think, therefore I am" (St. Pierre, 2000). Thus, the individual is conceived as an encapsulated body that has the ability to control outcomes, rather than a functioning element within a larger multiplicity producing change through the interaction of its parts. The Cartesian, human-centric perspective perpetuates the sense of being "endowed with a will, a freedom, an intentionality, which is then subsequently expressed in language, in action, in the public domain" (Butler, 1995, p. 136). When taken in the context of teaching, the human-centric perception translates into the expectation that teachers will be able to plan and execute instructional practice while "managing" or "controlling" students. With such an expectation, it is no wonder teachers experience extreme shock as they move into their first classrooms and encounter difficulty "transferring" their preservice learning (Cook, 2009; Huberman, 1989; Korthagen, Loughran, & Russell, 2006; Veenman, 1984).

Shifting from an "I", or individualistic, mentality to a more multiplistic perspective of teaching necessitates not only belief change, but also a fundamental shift in the way most individuals in our neoliberal society perceive the world. The commonsense logic with which the Western world operates is grounded in the idea that we are agentic beings with the individual power to control the world around us—an idea directly contradicted by the stories presented in this study that show the highly interactive, co-constructed nature of the teaching activity occurring in all three participants' classrooms. To help future teachers build awareness of the interrelated activity that will characterize their future teaching, we suggest that teacher educators attend to the negotiation process as a centerpiece of learning to teach. That is, teacher educators should give substantial attention to discussing the relational aspect of teaching and incorporating activities that highlight the agency of students and other actors in school settings, the power of historical and contextual discourses of education that shape teaching, and even the role of physical space and material objects in the production of teaching practice. For example, teacher candidates attending programs offering simultaneous coursework and clinical practice might implement an assignment where students plan and enact a lesson. Upon completion, the students could engage in a lesson reflection to identify all the forces (both human and nonhuman) that mediated the enactment of lesson, discuss how they negotiated these forces, and describe how these forces affected or influenced the intended instructional design.

For individuals receiving preparation with a clear division between coursework and field experiences, "approximations of practice" (Grossman, Compton, Igra, Ronfeldt, Shahan, & Williamson, 2009, p. 2076) that simulate learning situations may be helpful. For instance, students may be assigned to teach a lesson in pairs or small groups, and afterward the class might discuss particular pedagogical principles and how they were realized (or not) through the lesson. While such simulations may not provide teachers with the opportunity to discuss the navigation of various structural or other contextual constraints on their teaching, the exercises can highlight the collective processes of meaning-making the teacher engages in with her students during lessons.

As another way to illuminate the co-constructed nature of teaching, teacher educators should model the type of pedagogy teachers are expected to enact (Russell, 1999). Returning to the idea of belief change, most teacher candidates were taught in ways that align with transmission models of teaching—and as learners, most likely experienced success with this type of instruction (Richardson, 2003). To disrupt these traditional beliefs, future teachers must themselves experience learner-centered, collaborative instruction in the role of student (Villegas & Lucas, 2002). Beyond experiencing such instruction themselves as learners, future teachers must also have the opportunity to discuss and analyze teaching episodes from an instructional perspective to gain an understanding of the kind of in-the-moment co-construction that occurs in learner-centered teaching. As an example of how this might be operationalized in teacher education coursework, Berry and Loughran

(2002) offered their own instructional moves up for their students' critique, facilitating discussions about the pedagogical reasoning of the teacher. In a teacher education course dedicated to this type of learning experiences, the course leader might also draw attention to the ways that her teaching was modified in response to students' needs, participation, and reactions to further emphasize the collaborative nature of constructing practice.

Framing the work of the teacher as relational also offers the opportunity to re-examine more traditional notions about teaching from different angles. For example, new teachers frequently cite "classroom management" as one of their most pressing instructional concerns (Chubbock, 2008; Birrell, 1995; Romano, 2008; Hargreaves & Jacka, 1995; Veenman, 1984). Urban teachers often particularly struggle with maintaining order in the classroom (Milner & Tenore, 2010), for reasons Weiner (2003) illuminates in a review of research on classroom management in urban schools. For one, the schools themselves often do not offer support to teachers in building the type of environment or classroom culture needed to successful manage classrooms. Second, the frequent lack of alignment in cultural background between students and teachers in urban schools, as well as high mobility rates and other factors that contribute to environmental instability, may interfere with forming strong relationships, another important element in building a classroom community. Finally, deficit paradigms about students and custodian views of "managing" students are often so ingrained that teachers themselves do not recognize them.

Although some researchers have advocated for classroom management that works to address the social needs of culturally diverse students in urban schools (Brown, 2004; Milner & Tenore, 2010), the problem remains that the concept of "classroom management" itself is not a "culturally neutral" term, but rather a "white, middle-class construction" (Weinstein, 2004, p. 26). Further, the very language of classroom management invokes a managerial metaphor that echoes traditional authoritarian teacher roles. Despite the best intentions of teachers, the very ways in which we think about classroom management may reproduce discriminatory patterns and ignore cultural differences, which could be contributing factors to student resistance (Hand, 2010; Ogbu, 1986). In teacher education classrooms, we might purposefully seek to rupture this mode of thinking by inviting students of teaching to unpack the meaning and implications of "classroom management," interrogate their own beliefs and experiences with the construct, and try on new concepts that emphasize relational concepts of social interaction and community dynamics rather than control. Alongside such explorations, the cultural disconnects and power imbalances that may contribute to student resistance or oppositional behavior might be explicitly examined, as well as ways for teachers to negotiate power with students (Foucault, 1980; Brubaker, 2009) and support them in learning the rules of "the culture of power" (Delpit, 1988, p. 282).

PUTTING RHIZOMATICS TO WORK IN SCHOOLS

While it can be an important influence on teachers' instruction, preservice preparation is only one component of the teacher multiplicity, which in turn is only one part of the larger teaching-assemblage that collectively produces practice. As the three cases described in this study demonstrate, the school context provides multiple conditions and elements that have the power to shape teaching, and much of them contribute to the struggles of new teachers as they transition into their own classrooms. As Hargreaves and Jacka (1995) note, "It is clear that teacher education reform will continue to be a frustrating and futile endeavor until there is fundamental change in the cultures and contexts of schooling that beginning teachers encounter." For example, in contrast to many other professions, teachers are expected to take on all the same duties as seasoned veterans from the first day they set foot in their classrooms (Huling-Austin, 1996), despite the fact that they are still continuing to learn and develop (Feiman-Nemser, 2001). New teachers are also likely to receive the most difficult classes (Hargreaves & Jacka, 1995; Scherff, 2008; Tait, 2008), feel isolated and alone (Fantilli & McDougal, 2009; Griffin, Kilgore, & Winn, 2009; Stanulis, Fallona, & Pearson, 2002), and experience conflict between their pedagogical beliefs and those espoused by the administration, other teachers, and suggested by the school culture (Flores & Day, 2006; Chubbock et al., 2001; Sutherland, Saka, & Brooks, 2009).

The conditions noted above, combined with current neoliberal realities such as the systematic defunding of public schools, the proliferation of standardized testing, and the punitive turn of teacher evaluation, help make up the "overcoding" (Deleuze & Guattari, 1987) of the institution of schooling. These are molar lines, or forces that normalize teaching practice, that inhibit the enactment of practices grounded in social justice for multiple reasons, not least of which is new teachers' focus on their own professional survival (Chubbock, 2008). Although instructional leaders are constrained themselves within this system, they do have some agency to support new teachers. We argue that school leaders must become advocates for their first-year teachers, making use of the resources at their disposal—and working within their own molar lines—to help novices navigate the striated terrain of schools. The cases presented here, and in many other studies as well (e.g., Fry, 2007; Saka, Southerland, & Brooks, 2009; Scherff, 2008) provide clear examples of contextual conditions and school structures that both support and hinder new teachers as they attempt to construct a beginning pedagogy, and many of these are conditions and structures which school leaders themselves can affect if desired. For example, a school leader could ensure that new teachers are not assigned to teach lower-track or "remedial" courses, or they might help department chairs cultivate a professional learning community within a department to mediate isolation and increase collaboration among teachers.

Another area in which school and district leadership can provide further support involves induction and mentoring. Although two of the three teachers taking part

121

in this study reported their mentors were helpful in navigating issues in their first year of teaching, their mentoring situations generally matched those found in the novice teacher literature in terms of mismatch and inconsistent support (e.g., Castro, Kelly, & Shih, 2010; Fry, 2007; Stanulis, Fallona, & Pearson, 2002). Mauro's mentor taught a different branch of science—physics—and his induction coach was a retired English teacher. June's mentor was "non-existent," and her induction coach taught music part time. Bruce's mentor was a middle-school life science teacher with little physics content knowledge, and his induction coach was a retired second grade teacher who provided little support.

If the first year is, indeed, a critical time for the shaping of teaching practice and highly influential for teacher attrition (Smith & Ingersoll, 2004), districts and schools must invest in creating consistent and coherent induction programs that provide novice educators adequate supports. These include ensuring appropriate and qualified mentors (to help novice educators continue to develop their pedagogical learning) as well as helping them learn how to successfully and productively engage in the continual meaning-making processes, negotiations, and school site navigations that occur throughout the first year of practice. To do so, schools and districts have the responsibility to design and support induction programs that help teachers bridge the gap between their preservice learning and their instructional practices in their new settings. Specifically, induction programs should be designed with the knowledge that new teachers' biggest challenge is translating their pre-professional learning into practice amid all the different moving parts of their classroom and school. Such programs focused on the translation of pedagogy new teachers learned as part of their preservice preparation provide powerful possibilities for learning in and for practice (Lampert, 2010) or for using the teacher's current practices as the basis for learning, while also creating a community of support for them. For example, a mentor or induction coach might work with a group of new teachers to design an action research or inquiry cycle to investigate a problem of practice identified by each teacher. Focusing on this challenge, each teacher could formulate an initial plan to modify her own teaching, and collect data on the results of those modifications. After reflecting on the data, the induction group would reconvene and teachers would share their initial results with each other. Based on their preliminary results and dialogue, teachers would then return to the classroom to modify their practices again. However, access to this type of learning is not the norm in schools. For school and district leaders, endeavors to implement this kind of activity is yet another means of advocacy for new teachers.

PUTTING RHIZOMATICS TO WORK IN POLICY AND RESEARCH

In the final portion of this section, we offer implications for educational policy, as well as educational research, drawing on insights from our case studies and from the rhizomatic concepts we have discussed throughout this book. In particular, we suggest that educational policy efforts focused on accountability must press beyond reductionist, impoverished methods of assessing teachers and teacher preparation programs, methods which tend to focus on narrow outcomes obtained by questionable algorithms (Cochran-Smith, 2003). Similarly, we argue for a research agenda for preparing and supporting teachers that investigates teaching as complex phenomena, shifting from an outcomes-oriented, person-centered focus to emphasize the processes of teaching.

Educational Policy Regarding Teachers and Teacher Education

The educational policies of the United States are grounded in a positivistic, rationalist manner of thinking characterized by a belief in the complete autonomy of the individual and the unerring righteousness of capitalistic principles (Battram, 1998)—in short, the type of logic characterized by Deleuze and Guattari (1987) as arborescent thinking. Although such reductionist thought structures have long undergirded school norms such as the grade system that ranks students on an A-F scale, the separation of academic subjects into separate courses of study, and the traditional roles of the teacher and student, in the last decade an increasingly individualistic, neoliberal mode of thought in education policy has spawned an even more problematic agenda. Titled by some as "corporate education reform" (Karp, 2012; Ravitch, 2013), this label refers to both the market principles that inform related policies and the business interests funding the movement (Ravich, 2010, 2013).

One of the ways the corporate education reform agenda has insinuated itself into K-12 education is through "accountability" schemes that measure students for productivity and efficiency through various forms of high stakes testing (e.g., No Child Left Behind, 2002; Race to the Top, 2010). Although many scholars argue the tests are culturally and linguistically biased (e.g., Au, 2008; Darling-Hammond, 2007) and financial disparities between districts affect the resources available to prepare students to successfully pass them (Baker, Sciarra, Farrie, & Center, 2010), schools that do not meet particular achievement benchmarks on these tests are labeled as "failing" and subject to various sanctions (Lipman, 2004). As an extension of these policies, the Race to the Top initiative required states to develop evaluations providing for the quantitative assessment of teachers (Race to the Top, 2010). In response, several states have adopted policies that purport to hold teachers accountable for their performance by calculating their "value added" to their students, using a complex inferential statistic based on standardized test scores (Butrymowicz & Garland, 2012). Other states, like New Jersey, have begun using purely descriptive measures of student performance known as "Student Growth Outcomes" (SGOs) to make decisions about contract renewal, tenure, and dismissal (Baker, 2012).

With university-based teacher education under attack from proponents of the same corporate education movement (Zeichner, 2010b), it is not surprising that the accountability fervor has been extended to evaluating teacher preparation programs.

Specifically, policy-makers are exploring ways to hold teacher education programs responsible for the performance of their graduates by linking those institutions to their graduates' teaching evaluation scores (Knight, Edmonson, Lloyd, Arbaugh, Nolan, Whitney, & McDonald, 2012). Indeed, the 2011 "Our Future, our Teachers" report released by the Obama administration called for such a measure (U.S. Department of Education, 2011). While a discussion of the validity of these measures from a statistical perspective is beyond the scope of this book, the non-linear, collaboratively negotiated processes of constructing teaching practices demonstrated in this study suggest that focusing on an individual teacher through a single measurement, and by extension, their degree-granting university, is highly problematic. While each teacher's preservice learning was certainly an influence in the practices reported here, that knowledge was only one of many factors playing a part in the eventual production of instruction. These findings—which are consistent with research reported by others (e.g., Cochran-Smith, 2001; Davis & Sumara, 1997; Elmore, 2002; Opfer & Pedder, 2011; Starkey, 2010)—attest to the complex, nonlinear nature of teacher learning and practice, and suggest that evaluation schemes that equate teacher preparation program quality and individual teacher effectiveness with student test scores are unfounded (Cochran-Smith, 2003).

As several educational researchers have concluded, "value-added" and other reductionist, linear quantitative models of teacher and teacher preparation quality hold little or no value for actually informing teaching practice or the reform of teacher preparation programs at local levels (e.g., Cochran-Smith, Piazza, & Power, 2013; Zeichner, 2011). Rather than producing information which might help teachers, instructional leaders, teacher educators, and programs of teacher education to address important and insistent questions, these measures force its subjects into simplistic binaries of good/bad, right/wrong, failing/not failing, and so on (Cochran-Smith, 2003). Far from yielding important knowledge for the field of teaching and teacher preparation, instead quantitative outcomes-based evaluations of teacher preparation program and teacher quality produce skewed, black-and-white labels that serve little purpose other than to feed the neoliberal rhetoric of "accountability" at best (Cochran-Smith, Piazza, & Powers, 2013). At worst, these assessments support a deregulationist agenda of discrediting and dismantling teacher education and the public K-12 school system (Zeichner, 2003, 2010b).

Representing the complexity of teaching is a seemingly impossible task for many reasons, one of which is the conflux of elements occurring on multiple levels (teacher, classroom, school, district, state/federal). However, efforts are underway that attempt to produce more multifaceted evaluations of teaching practice for assessments of both individual teaching practice and teacher preparation programs. The Teacher Performance Assessment (TPA), a teacher evaluation system for initial certification created by the Performance Assessment for California Teachers' (PACT), is one such instrument (Merino & Pecheone, 2013). Taking a portfolio approach, the TPA assesses a battery of skills for beginning teachers, including lesson planning, implementation of practice, assessment of learning, and reflecting on instruction (Darling-Hammond, Newton, & Wei, 2013). A variety of sources, including video of lessons, lesson plans, written reflections, and student artifacts are used to assess these proficiencies. External evaluators score the portfolios, using rubrics containing descriptions of performance at four different levels (PACT, 2013). Drawing on PACT's model, the edTPA was developed as a national performance assessment of preservice teaching practice (Sato, 2014).

The TPA and edTPA, although currently intended only to evaluate preservice teaching, provide examples of a *more* nuanced assessment of teaching practice than current quantitative measures. However, there are still major problems with performance assessments such as these, including questions of context and the interactional aspects that shape teaching practice, as well as the outsourcing of teacher evaluations. Although PACT promises that its evaluators are extensively trained, highly experienced educational professionals (Darling-Hammond, Newton, & Wei, 2013), as does edTPA (edTPA, 2016), the evaluations are ultimately handled by a large, well-known for-profit educational corporation (Au, 2013). This raises numerous issues, including the ethics of giving a corporate entity the power to essentially grant teacher licensing and the loss of local control over certification decisions (Cochran-Smith, Piazza, & Powers, 2013). Moreover, external evaluators most likely have no contextual knowledge of the settings in which the teachers they are assessing are constructing their practice, making the likelihood that the ways in which the environment influences teaching will be considered basically nil. Because they lack this important knowledge of context, the focus of evaluations will be the teacher, and grading will occur via a rubric with pre-determined descriptions of quality practice. Thus, even these more in-depth and textured accounts of practice still position the teacher as an autonomous actor expected to perform in particular ways that are already prescribed. As Tuck and Gorlewski (2016) describe, "Wrapped in the rhetoric of professionalism and quality, edTPA represents the normalization of teaching as a technical and apolitical act, of examinations as meaningful measures of complex acts and useful instruments for surveillance and discipline, and of relationships and local contexts as subordinate to distant, objective expertise" (p. 203).

In addition to the issues that have been discussed above, the collective education policy world's preoccupation with the numerical measures of teacher and student performance raises another important concern in terms of accommodating the complexity of teaching in evaluating instructional practice. For qualitative measures such as the TPA or the commonly used *Framework for Teaching* (Danielson, 2007), assessment is ultimately performed via a rubric detailing decontextualized, predetermined "quality" practices. The prescribed nature of these tasks, and the specificity with which those predetermined practices are detailed, present little allowances for the translation of pedagogy. That translation entails a negotiation between the teacher, her students, and multiple contextual factors, indicating that pedagogy is not directly transferred into the classroom as a whole object, but rather is shaped simultaneously by the teacher and her assemblage through ongoing interaction. Thus, the product (teaching) may look different when translated into particular settings, which in turn may not fit neatly into one of the prescribed categories.

The issue of assessment for quality control is, itself (in Deleuzian terms), a molar line. The evaluation of programs and teachers for the purpose of determining who/which is good or bad is a structure intended to normalize among a particular set of predetermined criteria. Even within the qualitative measures designed to provide a richer picture of teaching, little room exists for difference or for true emergence—that is, the occurrence of something completely new, something that is not predictable from initial conditions, and perhaps even something which we do not yet know about. In their current forms, educational evaluation systems are *closed*. By virtue of their design, there is no new growth, no space for creativity, no room for new transformations at the local level (Mason, 2008; Davis & Sumara, 2006), because all the possibilities are already described. Instead, rather than expecting students of teacher education to perform practices with "high fidelity" (O'Donnell, 2008), we should design measures that can capture practices being performed with low fidelity because they are being contextually negotiated.

Research on Teaching

Alongside the accountability movement in K-12 and teacher education, the educational research community has experienced a resurgence of positivistic, quantitative research as the "gold standard" of quality research (St. Pierre, 2011). In fact, a 2004 Institute of Education Sciences (IES) report called for "a new generation of methodologically rigorous and educationally relevant research" that would counteract the profusion of qualitative research in education, which is "a clear sign of the mismatch between the focus of the practice community and the current research community" (Lather, 2006, citing IES, 2004). According to this report, psychometrics and statistics research is the only way to address persistent issues in education. Other reports and legislation in the last decade, such as No Child Left Behind's statement on quality research and the National Research Council's 2002 report, *Scientific Research in Education,* have echoed the calls for quantitative, mainly experimental research designs that perpetuate the "regime of truth" of objectivity and generalizability (Lincoln & Cannella, 2004).

In an era of both market-driven reforms and backlash against divergent forms of educational inquiry, designing and implementing studies that hold promise for investigating teaching as complex phenomena is more critical than ever. Non-linear methodological frameworks, such as thinking with rhizomatic concepts and situated analysis, move beyond "outcomes" and into the actual ontology of practice, turning researchers' attention to the processes that constitute teaching. The concepts we have used throughout this book offer ideas and language for thinking differently about teaching, highlighting and emphasizing the multiple, collaboratively constituted, and dynamic nature of teaching. Thinking with concepts like *assemblage, becoming, molar line, molecular line*, and *line of flight* as analytic tools opens up fossilized conceptualizations and modes of inquiring into teaching and promotes more complex understandings of enacting instructional practice.

Non-linear methodological approaches, such as those featured in this study, offer possibilities for conducting analyses that attend to connections among multiple elements in a setting, including those that are non-human, as well as the processes that shape the production of social activity (in this case, teaching). Using these methods—and other non-linear, systems-level approaches, such as Cultural-Historical Activity Theory (CHAT) and Actor-Network Theory—to conduct in-depth studies of teacher learning and practice can help provide critical resistance to both dominant research paradigms as well as programs that perpetuate an idea of teaching as executing a particular checklist of behaviors—and embrace a paradigm of difference over sameness. By highlighting the ontology of learning and practice—in other words, the way these processes are carried out, or the way learning moves across time and space into new teachers' classrooms—we can create a research agenda building evidence of the interactional, relational nature of teaching. To move the field forward, an ontological turn (Lather & St. Pierre, 2013) in teacher education research is needed, one specifically focusing on "how" questions and inquiries into the process of teaching.

Yet, to study teaching as non-linear phenomena, research frameworks are needed that can account for the phenomenon of *emergence,* or *becoming* (teaching occurrences that are entirely new and could not have been predicted from initial conditions). Computer simulations can now work to generate twenty-five possible scenarios for predicting how teachers will enact their learning (Opfer, 2013), but such an experiment is predicated on knowing all the possible outcomes. What if the practices that emerge or are collectively produced are something that is as yet unknown or un-imagined? Thus, we argue that we need more studies using rich, qualitative frameworks that can produce both thick descriptions (Geertz, 1973) and thick analysis (Clarke, 2003) showing the ongoing, dynamic, always-becoming nature of teaching at the classroom level. Specifically, studies that investigate interactions between teachers and students, and the ways that multiple classroom-level elements shape teaching practice, are needed.

REFERENCES

Achinstein, B., & Ogawa, R. (2011). *Change(d) agents: New teachers of color in urban schools.* New York, NY: Teachers College Press.

Achinstein, B., Ogawa, R., & Speiglman, A. (2004). Are we creating separate and unequal tracks of teachers? The effects of state policy, local conditions, and teacher characteristics on teacher socialization. *American Educational Research Journal, 41*(3), 557–603. doi:10.3102/00028312041003557

Adler, P. A., & Adler, P. (1998). *Membership roles in field research.* Thousand Oaks, CA: Sage.

Albrecht-Crane, C., & Slack, J. (2003). Toward a pedagogy of affect. In J. Slack (Ed.), *Animations of Deleuze & Guattari* (pp. 191–216). New York, NY: Peter Lang.

Allan, J. (2011). Complicating not explicating: Taking up philosophy in learning disability research. *Learning Disability Quarterly, 34*(2), 153–161. doi:10.1177/073194871103400206

Allebone, B. (2006). Who should I put in a circle group? Influences on the practice of beginning teachers: A small study. *Education, 3-13, 34*(2), 131–141. doi:10.1080/03004270600670490

Allen, J. (2009). Valuing practice over theory: How beginning teachers reorient their practice in the transition from university to workplace. *Teaching & Teacher Education, 25*(5), 647–654. doi:10.1016/j.tate.2008.11.011

Andersson, I., & Andersson, S. (2008). Conditions for boundary crossing: Social practices of newly qualified Swedish teachers. *Scandinavian Journal of Educational Research, 52*(6), 643–660. doi:10.1080/00313830802497307

Apple, M., & Beane, J. (1995). *Democratic schools.* Alexandria, VA: Association for Supervision and Curriculum Development.

Au, W. (2008). *Unequal by design: High stakes testing and the standardization of inequality.* New York, NY: Routledge.

Au, W. (2013). What's a nice test like you doing in a place like this? The edTPA and corporate education "Reform". *Rethinking Schools, 27*(4), 22–27.

Au, W., Karp, S., & Bigelow, B. (2007). *Rethinking our classrooms: Teaching for equity and justice* (Rev. ed.). Milwaukee, WI: Rethinking Schools.

Baines, L. (2010). *The teachers we need vs. the teachers we have.* Lanham, MD: Rowman & Littlefield.

Baker, B. (2012). *Take your SGPs and VAMit, damn it!* Retrieved from http://schoolfinance101.wordpress.com/2011/09/02/take-your-sgp-and-vamit-damn-it/

Baker, B. D., Sciarra, D. G., & Farrie, D. (2010). *Is school funding fair? A national report card.* Newark, NJ: Education Law Center.

Banks, J., Cochran-Smith, C., Moll, L., Richert, Zeichner, K., LaPage, P., Darling-Hammond, L., Huffy, H., & McDonald, M. (2005). Teaching diverse learners. In L. Darling-Hammond & J. Bransford (Eds.), *Preparing teachers for a changing world: What teachers should learn and be able to do* (pp. 232–274). San Francisco, CA: Jossey-Bass.

Barad, K. (2007). *Meeting the universe halfway.* Durham, NC: Duke University Press.

Battram, A. (1998). *Navigating complexity.* London, UK: The Industrial Society.

Beck, C., Kosnik, C., & Roswell, J. (2007). Preparation for the first year of teaching: Beginning teachers' views about their needs. *The New Educator, 3*(1), 51–73. doi:10.1080/15476880601141581

Beijaard, D., Meijer, P. C., & Verloop, N. (2004). Reconsidering research on teachers' professional identity. *Teaching and Teacher Education, 20*(2), 107–128. doi:10.1016/j.tate.2003.07.001

Belenky, M., Clinchy, B., Goldberger, N., & Tarule, J. (1997). *Women's ways of knowing: Development of voice, self, and mind* (10th anniversary edition). New York, NY: Basic Books.

Bergeron, B. (2008). Enacting a culturally responsive curriculum in a novice teacher's classroom: Encountering disequilibrium. *Urban Education, 43*(4), 4–28. doi:10.1177/0042085907309208

Berliner, D. (1988). Teacher expertise. In B. Moon & A. Mayes (Eds.), *Teaching and learning in the secondary school* (pp. 107–113). New York, NY: Routledge.

Berry, B., Montgomery, D., & Snyder, J. (2008). *Urban teacher residency models at institutes of higher education: Implications for teacher preparation.* New York, NY: Center for Teaching Quality.

Bhabha, H. K. (1994). *The location of culture*. London, UK: Routledge.

Bianchini, J., & Cazavos, L. (2007). Learning from students, inquiry into practice, and participation in professional communities: Beginning teachers' uneven progress toward equitable science teaching. *Journal of Research in Science Teaching, 44*(4), 586–612. doi:10.1002/tea.20177

Birrell, J. (1995). Learning how the game is played: A beginning teacher's struggle to prepare black youth for a white world. *Teaching and Teacher Education, 11*(2), 137–147. doi:10.1002/tea.20177

Black, A., & Ammon, P. (1992). A developmental-constructivist approach to teacher education. *Journal of Teacher Education, 43*(5), 323–335. doi:10.1177/0022487192043005002

Blackman, L. (2012). *Immaterial bodies: Affect, embodiment, mediation*. London, UK: Sage.

Bourdieu, P. (1973). *Knowledge, education, and cultural change*. London, UK: Harper & Row Publishers.

Brashier, A., & Norris, E. (2008). Breaking down barriers for first year teachers: What teacher education preparation programs can do. *Journal of Early Childhood Teacher Education, 29*(1), 30–44. doi:10.1080/10901020701878651

Britzman, D. (1991). *Practice makes practice: A critical study of learning to teach*. Albany, NY: State University of New York Press.

Brown, D. F. (2004). Urban teachers' professed classroom management strategies reflections of culturally responsive teaching. *Urban Education, 39*(3), 266–289. doi:10.1177/0042085904263258

Brubaker, N. D. (2010). Negotiating authority by designing individualized grading contracts. *Studying Teacher Education, 6*(3), 257–267. Retrieved from http://www.jstor.org/stable/23479286

Bullough, R. V. (1997). Becoming a teacher: Self and the social location of teacher education. In B. Biddle, T. Good, & I. Goodson (Eds.), *International handbook of teachers and teaching* (pp. 79–134). Dordrecht, Netherlands: Springer.

Bullough, R. (2005). The quest for identity in teaching and teacher education. In G. Hoban (Ed.), *The missing links in teacher education design* (pp. 237–258). Dordrecht, The Netherlands: Springer.

Bullough, R., & Draper, R. J. (2004). Making sense of a failed triad: Mentors, university supervisors, and positioning theory. *Journal of Teacher Education, 55*(5), 407–420. doi:10.1177/0022487104269804

Butler, J. (1995). For a careful reading. In S. Benhabib, J. Butler, D. Cornell, & N. Fraser (Eds.), *Feminist contentions: A philosophical exchange* (pp. 127–143). London, UK: Routledge.

Butrymowicz, S., & Garland, S. (2012). *New York city teacher ratings: How its value-added model compares to other districts*. Retrieved from http://www.huffingtonpost.com/2012/03/02/new-york-city-teacher-rat_n_1316755.html

Cady, J., Meier, S., & Lubinski, C. (2006). Developing mathematics teachers: The transition from preservice to experienced teacher. *Journal of Educational Research, 99*(5), 295–305. doi:10.3200/JOER.99.5.295-306

Castro, A., Kelly, J., & Shih, M. (2010). Resilience strategies for new teachers in high-needs areas. *Teaching and Teacher Education, 26*(1), 622–629. doi:10.1016/j.tate.2009.09.010

Charmaz, K. (2006). *Constructing grounded theory: A practical guide through qualitative analysis*. London, UK: Sage.

Charmaz, K. (2011). Grounded theory methods in social justice research. In N. Denzin & Y. Lincoln (Eds.), *The Sage handbook of qualitative research* (4th ed., pp. 359–380). Thousand Oaks, CA: Sage.

Chin, E., Young, J., & Floyd, B. (2004, March 4). *Placing beginning teachers in hard to staff schools: Dilemmas posed by alternative certification programs*. Paper presented at the American Association of Colleges of Teacher Education (AACTE), Chicago, IL.

Chubbuck, S. (2008). A novice teacher's beliefs about socially just teaching: Dialogue of many voices. *The New Educator, 4*(4), 309–329. doi:10.1080/15476880802430254

Chubbuck, S., Clift, R., Allard, J., & Quinlan, J. (2001). Playing it safe as a novice teacher: Implications for programs for new teachers. *Journal of Teacher Education, 52*(5), 365–376. doi:10.1080/15476880802430254

City, E. A., Elmore, R. F., Fiarman, S. E., & Teitel, L. (2009). *Instructional rounds in education: A network approach to improving teaching and learning*. Cambridge, MA: Harvard Education Press.

Clarke, A. (2003). Situational analyses: Grounded theory mapping after the postmodern turn. *Symbolic Interaction, 26*(4), 553–576. doi:10.1525/si.2003.26.4.553

Clarke, A. (2005). *Situational analysis: Grounded theory after the postmodern turn*. Thousand Oaks, CA: Sage.

Clarke, A., & Collins, S. (2007). Complexity science and student teacher supervision. *Teaching and Teacher Education, 23*(2), 160–172. doi:10.1016/j.tate.2006.10.006

Cochran-Smith, M. (2003). The unforgiving complexity of teaching: Avoiding simplicity in the age of accountability. *Journal of Teacher Education, 54*(1), 3–5. doi:10.1177/0022487102238653

Cochran-Smith, M. (2004). *Walking the road: Race, diversity, and social justice in teacher education.* New York, NY: Teachers College Press.

Cochran-Smith, M., & Lytle, S. L. (1999). Relationships of knowledge and practice: Teacher learning in communities. *Review of Research in Education, 24*, 294–305. Retrieved from http://www.jstor.org/stable/1167272

Cochran-Smith, M., Shakman, K., Jong, C., Terrell, D. G., Barnatt, J., & McQuillan, P. (2009). Good and just teaching: The case for social justice in teacher education. *American Journal of Education, 115*(3), 347–377. doi:10.1086/597493

Cochran-Smith, M., Piazza, P., & Power, C. (2013). The politics of accountability: Assessing teacher education in the United States. *The Educational Forum, 77*(1), 6–27. doi:10.1080/00131725.2013.739015

Cochran-Smith, M., Ell, F., Ludlow, L., Grudnoff, L., & Aitken, G. (2014). The challenge and promise of complexity theory for teacher education research. *Teachers College Record, 116*(5), 1–38.

Cochran-Smith, M., Villegas, A. M., Abrams, L., Chavez Moreno, L., Mills, T., & Stern, R. (2016). Research on teacher preparation: Charting the process of a sprawling field. In D. Gitomer & C. Bell (Eds.), *Handbook of research on teaching* (pp. 439–548). Washington, DC: AERA.

Cohen, D. (1988). Teaching practice: Plus que ca change.... In P. W. Jackson (Ed.), *Contributing to educational change* (pp. 27–84). Berkeley, CA: McCutchan Publishing.

Colebrook, C. (2002). *Understanding Deleuze.* New York, NY: Routledge.

Coleman, R., & Ringrose, J. (Eds.). (2013). *Deleuze and research methodologies.* Edinburgh: Edinburgh University Press.

Cook, J. (2009). "Coming into my own as a teacher": Identity, disequilibrium, and the first year of teaching. *The New Educator, 5*(4), 274–292. doi:10.1080/1547688X.2009.10399580

Costa, A., & Kallick, B. (1993). Through the lens of a critical friend. *Educational Leadership, 51*(2), 49–51.

Cummins, J. (2000). *Language, power, and pedagogy: Bilingual children in the crossfire.* Clevedon, UK: Multilingual Matters.

Danielson, C. (2007). *Enhancing professional practice: A framework for teaching.* Alexandria, VA: Association for Supervision and Curriculum Development.

Darling-Hammond, L. (1990). Teaching and knowledge: Policy issues posed by alternate certification for teachers. *Peabody Journal of Education, 67*(3), 123–154. doi:10.1080/01619569009538694

Darling-Hammond, L. (1996). The right to learn and the advancement of teaching: Research, policy, and practice for democratic education. *Educational Researcher, 25*(6), 5–17. Retrieved from http://www.jstor.org/stable/1176043

Darling-Hammond, L. (1997). *The right to learn: A blueprint for creating schools that work.* San Francisco, CA: Jossey-Bass.

Darling-Hammond, L. (2006). Constructing 21st century teacher education. *Journal of Teacher Education, 57*(3), 300–314. doi:10.1177/0022487105285962

Darling-Hammond, L. (2007). Race, inequality and educational accountability: The irony of 'No Child Left Behind'. *Race Ethnicity and Education, 10*(3), 245–260. doi:10.1080/13613320701503207

Darling-Hammond, L. (2010). *The flat world and education: How America's commitment to equity will determine our future.* New York, NY: Teachers College Press.

Darling-Hammond, L., & Bransford, J. (2005). *Preparing teachers for a changing world: What teachers should learn and be able to do.* San Francisco, CA: Jossey-Bass.

Darling-Hammond, L., Newton, S. P., & Wei, R. C. (2013). Developing and assessing beginning teacher effectiveness: The potential of performance assessments. *Educational Assessment, Evaluation and Accountability, 25*(3), 179–204. doi:10.1007/s11092-013-9163-0

Davis, B., & Sumara, D. J. (1997). Cognition, complexity, and teacher education. *Harvard Educational Review, 67*(1), 105–126. doi:10.1007/s11092-013-9163-0

REFERENCES

Davis, B., & Sumara, D. (2006). *Complexity and education: Inquiries into learning, teaching and research*. London, UK: Lawrence Erlbaum.

de Freitas, E. (2012). Classroom as rhizome: New strategies for diagramming knotted interactions. *Qualitative Inquiry, 18*(7), 557–570. doi:10.1177/1077800412450155

Deleuze, G. (1987). *A Thousand plateaus: Capitalism and schizophrenia* (Vol. 2). Minneapolis, MN: University of Minnesota Press.

Deleuze, G. (1990). *The logic of sense*. New York, NY: Columbia University Press.

Deleuze, G. (1995). *Negotiations 1972–1990*. New York, NY: Columbia University Press.

Deleuze, G., & Guattari, F. (1983). *Anti-Oedipus: Capitalism and schizophrenia*. Minneapolis, MN: University of Minnesota Press.

Delpit, L. (2006). *Other people's children: Cultural conflict in the classroom* (2nd ed.). New York, NY: New Press.

Delpit, L. D. (1988). The silenced dialogue: Power and pedagogy in educating other people's children. *Harvard Educational Review, 58*(3), 280–298. doi:10.17763/haer.58.3.c43481778r528qw4

Dewey, J. (1925). *Experience and nature*. New York, NY: Dover.

Dewey, J. (1938). *Experience and education*. New York, NY: Collier MacMillan.

Dyke, S. (2013). Disrupting anorexia nervosa: An ethnography of the Deleuzian event. In F. Colman & J. Ringrose (Eds.), *Deleuze and research methodologies* (pp. 145–163). Edinburgh, UK: Edinburgh University Press.

Eakle, A. J. (2007). Literacy spaces of a Christian faith-based school. *Reading Research Quarterly, 42*(4), 472–510. doi:10.1598/RRQ.42.4.3

Eldar, E., Nabel, N., Schechter, C., Tamor, R., & Mazin, K. (2003). Anatomy of success and failure: The story of three novice teachers. *Educational Research, 45*(1), 29–48. doi:10.1080/0013188032000086109

Ellingson, L. (2009). *Engaging in crystallization in qualitative research: An introduction*. Thousand Oaks, CA: Sage.

Elmore, R. F. (2002). Hard questions about practice. *Educational Leadership, 59*(8), 22–25.

Fantilli, R., & McDougal, D. (2009). A study of novice teachers: Challenges and supports in the first years. *Teaching and Teacher Education, 25*(4), 814–825. doi:10.1016/j.tate.2009.02.021

Farrell, T. (2003). Learning to teach English during the first year: Personal influences and challenges. *Teaching and Teacher Education, 19*(1), 95–111. doi:10.1016/S0742-051X(02)00088-4

Feiman-Nemser, S. (1993). *Teacher mentoring: A critical review*. Washington, DC: ERIC Clearinghouse on Teaching and Teacher Education.

Feiman-Nemser, S. (2001). From preparation to practice: Designing a continuum to support and sustain practice. *Teacher's College Record, 103*(6), 1013–1055.

Feiman-Nemser, S., & Buchmann, M. (1985). Pitfalls of experience in teacher preparation. *Teachers College Record, 87*(1), 255–273.

Ferguson-Patrick, K. (2011). Professional development of early career teachers: A pedagogical focus on collaborative learning. *Issues in Education, 21*(2), 109–129.

Flores, M., & Day, C. (2006). Contexts which shape and reshape new teachers' identities: A multi-perspective study. *Teaching and Teacher Education, 22*(1), 219–232. doi:10.1016/j.tate.2005.09.002

Foucault, M. (1976). *Discipline and punish: The birth of the prison*. New York, NY: Random House.

Foucault, M. (1980). Truth and power. In C. Gordon (Ed.), *Power/Knowledge: Selected interviews and other writings, 1972–1977*. New York, NY: Pantheon Books.

Freire, P. (1970). *Pedagogy of the oppressed*. New York, NY: Continuum.

Freire, P. (1998). *Pedagogy of freedom: Ethics, democracy, and civic courage*. Lanham, MD: Rowman & Littlefield.

Freire, P., & Macedo, D. (1987). *Literacy: Reading the word and the world*. Westport, CT: Bergin & Garvey.

Fry, S. (2007). First-year teachers and induction support: Ups, downs, and in-betweens. *The Qualitative Report, 12*(2), 216–237. Retrieved from http://nsuworks.nova.edu/tqr/vol12/iss2/6

Fuller, F. (1969). Concerns of teachers: A developmental conceptualization. *American Educational Research Journal, 6*(2), 207–226. Retrieved from http://www.jstor.org/stable/1161894

Garrett, K. C. (2013). Teach for America, urban reform, and the New Taylorism in education. In P. Thomas (Ed.), *Becoming and being a teacher: Confronting traditional norms to create new democratic realities* (pp. 27–42). New York, NY: Peter Lang.

Geertz, C. (1973). *The interpretation of cultures: Selected essays.* New York, NY: Basic books.

Gibbons, P. (2002). *Scaffolding language, scaffolding learning: Teaching second language learners in the mainstream classroom.* Portsmouth, NH: Heinemann.

Giroux, H. A. (2002). Critical theory and educational practice. In A. Darder, M. Torres, & R. Baltodano (Eds.), *The critical pedagogy reader* (2nd ed., pp. 364–383). New York, NY: Routledge.

González, N., Moll, L. C., & Amanti, C. (Eds.). (2006). *Funds of knowledge: Theorizing practices in households, communities, and classrooms.* New York, NY: Routledge.

Goodley, D. (2007). Towards socially just pedagogies: Deleuzoguattarian critical disability studies. *International Journal of Inclusive Education, 11*(3), 317–334. doi:10.1080/13603110701238769

Grant, C. (2012). Cultivating flourishing lives: A robust social justice vision of education. *American Educational Research Journal, 49*(5), 910–934. doi:10.3102/0002831212447977

Griffin, C. C., Kilgore, K. L., Winn, J. A., Otis-Wilborn, A., Hou, W., & Garvan, C. W. (2009). First-year special educators: The influence of school and classroom context factors on their accomplishments and problems. *Teacher Education and Special Education, 32*(1), 45–63. doi:10.1177/0888406408330870

Grossman, P., Compton, C., Igra, D., Ronfeldt, M., Shahan, E., & Williamson, P. (2009). Teaching practice: A cross-professional perspective. *Teachers College Record, 111*(9), 2055–2100.

Grossman, P., Hammerness, K., & McDonald, M. (2009). Redefining teaching, re-imagining teacher education. *Teachers and Teaching: Theory and Practice, 15*(2), 273–289. doi:10.1080/13540600902875340

Haberman, M. (1995). *Star teachers of children in poverty.* West Lafayette, IN: Kappa Delta Phi.

Haberman, M. (2010). *Star teachers of children in poverty.* West Lafayette, IN: Kappa Delta Phi.

Hand, V. M. (2010). The co-construction of opposition in a low-track mathematics classroom. *American Educational Research Journal, 47*(1), 97–132. doi:10.3102/0002831209344216

Hargreaves, A., & Jacka, N. (1995). Induction or seduction? Postmodern patterns of preparing to teach. *Peabody Journal of Education, 70*(3), 41–63. doi:10.1080/01619569509538834

He, Y., & Cooper, J. (2011). Struggles and strategies in teaching: Voices of five novice secondary teachers. *Teacher Education Quarterly, 38*(2), 97–116. doi:10.1016/S0742-051X(01)00039-7

Hebert, E., & Worthy, T. (2001). Does the first year of teaching have to be a bad one? A case study of success. *Teaching and Teacher Education, 17*(8), 897–911. doi:10.1016/S0742-051X(01)00039-7

Hinchey, P. (1998). *Finding freedom in the classroom: A practical introduction to critical theory.* New York, NY: Peter Lang.

Hollingworth, S. (1992). Learning to teach through collaborative conversation: A feminist approach. *American Educational Research Journal, 29*(2), 373–404. doi:10.3102/00028312029002373

Huberman, M. (1989). The professional life cycle of teachers. *Teacher's College Record, 91*(1), 31–81.

Huling-Austin, L. (1992). Research on learning to teach: Implications for teacher induction and mentoring programs. *Journal of Teacher Education, 43*(3), 173–180. doi:10.1177/0022487192043003003

Humphrey, D. C., & Wechsler, M. E. (2007). Insights into alternative certification: Initial findings from a national study. *Teachers College Record, 109*(3), 483–530.

Ingersoll, R. M. (2003). *Is there really a teacher shortage? A research report.* Seattle, WA: Center for the Study of Teaching and Policy.

Jackson, A. Y., & Mazzei, L. (2012). *Thinking with theory in qualitative research: Using epistemological frameworks in the production of meaning.* New York, NY: Routledge.

Karp, S. (2012). *Challenging corporate reform, and ten hopeful signs of resistance.* Retrieved July 11, 2012, from http://www.rethinkingschools.org

Kilgore, K., Ross, D., & Zbikowski, J. (1990), Understanding the teaching perspectives of first-year teachers. *Journal of Teacher Education, 41*(1), 28–38. doi:10.1177/002248719004100105

Kincheloe, J. L. (2001). Describing the bricolage: Conceptualizing a new rigor in qualitative research. *Qualitative inquiry, 7*(6), 679–692. doi:10.1177/107780040100700601

Kincheloe, J. L. (2005). On to the next level: Continuing the conceptualization of the bricolage. *Qualitative inquiry, 11*(3), 323–350. doi:10.1177/1077800405275056

Klein, E. J., Taylor, M., Onore, C., Strom, K., & Abrams, L. (2013). Finding a third space in teacher education: Creating an urban teacher residency with Montclair State University and the Newark public schools. *Teaching Education, 24*(1), 27–57. doi:10.1080/10476210.2012.711305

Knight, S. L., Edmondson, J., Lloyd, G. M., Arbaugh, F., Nolan, J., Whitney, A. E., & McDonald, S. P. (2012). Examining the complexity of assessment and accountability in teacher education. *Journal of Teacher Education, 63*(5), 301–303. doi:10.1177/0022487112460200

Korthagen, F. A., & Kessels, J. P. (1999). Linking theory and practice: Changing the pedagogy of teacher education. *Educational Researcher, 28*(4), 4–17. doi:10.3102/0013189X028004004

Korthagen, F., Loughran, J., & Russell, T. (2006). Developing fundamental principles for teacher education programs and practices. *Teaching and Teacher Education, 22*(8), 1020–1041. doi:10.1207/s15326985ep2701_6

Ladson-Billings, G. (1994). *The dreamkeepers: Successful teachers of African-American children.* San Francisco, CA: Jossey-Bass.

Ladson-Billings, G. (1995). Toward a theory of culturally relevant pedagogy. *American Educational Research Journal, 32*(3), 465–491. doi:10.3102/00028312032003465

Lambson, D. (2010). Novice teachers learning through participation in a teacher study group. *Teaching and Teacher Education, 26*(8), 1660–1668. doi:10.1016/j.tate.2010.06.017

Lampert, M. (2010). Learning teaching in, from, and for practice: What do we mean? *Journal of Teacher Education, 61*(1–2), 21–34. doi:10.1177/0022487109347321

Lasky, S. (2005). A sociocultural approach to understanding teacher identity, agency and professional vulnerability in a context of secondary school reform. *Teaching and Teacher Education, 21*(8), 899–916. doi:10.1016/j.tate.2005.06.003

Lather, P. (1993). Fertile obsession: Validity after poststructuralism. *Sociological Quarterly, 34*(4), 673–693. doi:10.1111/j.1533-8525.1993.tb00112.x

Lather, P. (2006). Paradigm proliferation as a good thing to think with: Teaching research in education as a wild profusion. *International Journal of Qualitative Studies in Education, 19*(1), 35–57. doi:10.1080/09518390500450144

Lather, P., & St. Pierre, E. A. (2013). Post-qualitative research. *International Journal of Qualitative Studies in Education, 26*(6), 629–633. doi:10.1080/09518398.2013.788752

Lincoln, Y. S., & Cannella, G. S. (2004). Dangerous discourses: Methodological conservatism and governmental regimes of truth. *Qualitative Inquiry, 10*(1), 5–14. doi: 10.1177/1077800403259717

Lincoln, Y. S., & Guba, E. (1985). *Naturalistic inquiry.* Newbury Park, CA: Sage.

Lipman, P. (2004). Beyond accountability. In A. Darder, M. Torres, & R. Baltodano (Eds.), *The critical pedagogy reader* (2nd ed, pp. 364–383). New York, NY: Routledge.

Lipman, P. (2011). *The new political economy of education: Neoliberalism, race, and the right to the city.* New York, NY: Routledge.

Löfström, E., & Eisenschmidt, E. (2009). Novice teachers' perspectives on mentoring: The case of the Estonian induction year. *Teaching and Teacher Education, 25*(5), 681–689. doi:10.1016/j.tate.2008.12.005

Lortie, D. (1975). *Schoolteacher: A sociological study.* Chicago, IL: University of Chicago Press.

Lucas, T. (2011). *Teacher preparation for linguistically diverse classrooms: A resource for teacher educators.* New York, NY: Routledge.

Lucas, T., & Villegas, A. M. (2013). Preparing linguistically responsive teachers: Laying the foundation in preservice teacher education. *Theory Into Practice, 52*(2), 98–109. doi:10.1080/00405841.2013.770327

Lucas, T., Villegas, A. M., & Freedson-Gonzalez, M. (2008). Linguistically responsive teacher education: Preparing classroom teachers to teach English language learners. *Journal of Teacher Education, 59*(4), 361–373. doi:10.1177/0022487108322110

Luft, J., & Roehrig, G. (2005). Enthusiasm is not enough: Beginning secondary science teachers in primarily Hispanic settings. *School Science & Mathematics, 105*(3), 116–127. doi:10.1111/j.1949-8594.2005.tb18046.x

MacLure, M. (2013). Classification or wonder? Coding as analytic practice in qualitative research. In R. Coleman & J. Ringrose (Eds.), *Deleuze and research methodologies* (pp. 164–183). Edinburgh, UK: Edinburgh University Press.

Martin, A. D., & Kamberelis, G. (2013). Mapping not tracing: Qualitative educational research with political teeth. *International Journal of Qualitative Studies in Education, 26*(6), 668–679. doi:10.1080/09518398.2013.788756

Mason, M. (2008). Complexity theory and the philosophy of education. In M. Mason (Ed.), *Complexity theory and the philosophy of education* (pp. 46–61). Chichester, UK: Wiley-Blackwell.

Massengill, D., Mahlios, M., & Barry, A. (2005). Metaphors and sense of teaching: How these constructs influence novice teachers. *Teaching Education, 16*(3), 213–229. doi:10.1080/10476210500204887

Mathieson, S. (1988). Why triangulate? *Educational Researcher, 17*(2), 13–17. doi:10.3102/0013189X017002013

McAlpine, L., & Crago, M. (1995). The induction year experience in a cross-cultural setting. *Teaching and Teacher Education, 11*(4), 403–415. doi:10.1016/0742-051X(95)00009-9

McDonald, J., Mohr, N., Dichter, A., & McDonald, E. (2003). *The power of protocols: An educator's guide to improving practice.* New York, NY: Teacher's College Press.

McDonough, K. (2009). Pathways to critical consciousness: A first-year teacher's engagement with issues of race and equity. *Journal of Teacher Education, 60*(5), 528–537. doi:10.1177/0022487109348594

McElhone, D., Hebard, H., Scott, R., & Juel, C. (2009). The role of vision in trajectories of literacy practice among new teachers. *Studying Teacher Education, 5*(2), 147–158. doi:10.1080/17425960903306682

McNiff, J., Lomax, P., & Whitehead, J. (1996). *You and your action research project.* New York, NY: Routledge.

Merino, N., & Pecheone, R. (2013). The performance assessment for California teachers: An introduction. *The New Educator, 9*(1), 3–11. doi:10.1080/1547688X.2013.751310

Merriam S. (2009). *Qualitative research: A guide to design and implementation* (3rd ed.). San Francisco, CA: Jossey-Bass.

Miles, M., & Huberman, A. (1994). *Qualitative data analysis: An expanded sourcebook* (2nd ed.). Thousand Oaks, CA: Sage.

Milner, H. R., & Tenore, F. B. (2010). Classroom management in diverse classrooms. *Urban Education, 45*(5), 560–603. doi:10.1177/0042085910377290

Newman, E. (2010). 'I'm being measured as an NQT, that isn't who I am': An exploration of the experiences of career changer primary teachers in their first year of teaching. *Teachers and Teaching: Theory and Practice, 16*(4), 461–475. doi:10.1080/13540601003754830

Nieto, S. (2000). Placing equity front and center: Some thoughts on transforming teacher education for a new century. *Journal of Teacher education, 51*(3), 180–187. doi:10.1177/0022487100051003004

O'Donnell, C. L. (2008). Defining, conceptualizing, and measuring fidelity of implementation and its relationship to outcomes in K–12 curriculum intervention research. *Review of Educational Research, 78*(1), 33–84. doi:10.3102/0034654307313793

Ogbu, J. (1982). Cultural discontinuities and schooling. *Anthropology and Education Quarterly, 13*(4), 290–307. doi:10.1525/aeq.1982.13.4.05x1505w

Ogbu, J. U. (1986). The consequences of the American caste system. In U. Neisser (Ed.), *The school achievement of minority children: New perspectives* (pp. 19–56). Mahwah, NJ: Lawrence Earlbaum.

Olsen, B. (2008). Reasons for entry into the profession illuminate teacher identity development. *Teacher Education Quarterly, 35*(3), 23–40. Retrieved from http://www.jstor.org/stable/23478979

Opfer, D. (2013). *Methodological implications of a complexity theory-based approach to understanding teacher learning.* Paper presented at the American Educational Research Association annual meeting in San Francisco, CA.

Opfer, V., & Pedder, D. (2011). Conceptualizing teacher professional learning. *Review of Educational Research, 81*(3), 376–407. doi:10.3102/0034654311413609

Ovens, A., Strom, K., & Garbett, D. (2016). *A rhizomatic reading of becoming-teacher educator.* Paper presented at the Self-Study of Teacher Education Practices biennial conference in East Sussex, England.

Pajares, M. F. (1992). Teacher beliefs: Cleaning up a messy construct. *Review of Educational Research, 62*(3), 307–332. doi:10.3102/00346543062003307

Patton, M. (1990). *Qualitative evaluation and research methods.* Newbury Park, CA: Sage.

Ravitch, D. (2010). *The life and death of the great American school system.* New York, NY: Basic.

Ravitch, D. (2013). *Reign of error: The hoax of the privatization movement and the danger to America's public schools.* New York, NY: Random House.

Richardson, L. (1994). Writing: A method of inquiry. In N. Denzin & Y. Lincoln (Eds.), *Handbook of qualitative research* (pp. 516–529). Thousand Oaks, CA: Sage.

Richardson, V. (1996). The role of attitudes and beliefs in learning to teach. In J. Sikula (Ed.), *Handbook of research on teacher education* (2nd ed, pp. 102–119). New York, NY: MacMillan.

Richardson, V. (2003). Preservice teachers' beliefs. *Teacher Beliefs and Classroom Performance: The Impact of Teacher Education, 6*, 1–22.

Rodgers, C. R., & Scott, K. H. (2008). The development of the personal self and professional identity in learning to teach. In M. Cochran-Smith, S. Feiman-Nemser, D. J. McIntyre, & K. E. Demers (Eds.), *Handbook of research on teacher education* (pp. 732–755). New York, NY: Routledge.

Romano, M. (2008). Struggles of the beginning teacher: Widening the sample. *The Educational Forum, 72*(1), 63–78. doi:10.1080/00131720701603651

Romano, M., & Gibson, P. (2006). Beginning teacher successes and struggles: An elementary teacher's reflections on the first year of teaching. *The Professional Educator, 28*(1), 1–16.

Roy, K. (2003). *Teachers in nomadic spaces*. New York, NY: Peter Lang.

Rushton, S. P. (2001). Cultural assimilation: A narrative case study of student-teaching in an inner-city school. *Teaching and Teacher Education, 17*(2), 147–160. doi:10.1016/S0742-051X(00)00048-2

Saka, Y., Southerland, S., & Brooks, J. (2009). Becoming a member of a school community while working toward science education reform: Teacher induction from a cultural historical activity theory (CHAT) perspective. *Science Education, 93*(6), 996–1025. doi:10.1002/sce.20342

Sato, M. (2014). What is the underlying conception of teaching of the edTPA?. *Journal of Teacher Education, 65*(5), 412–434. doi:10.1177/0022487114542518

Schapiro, B. (2009). Negotiating a third space in the classroom. *Pedagogy, 9*(3), 423–439. doi:10.1215/15314200-2009-004

Scherff, L. (2008). Disavowed: The stories of two novice teachers. *Teaching and Teacher Education, 24*(5), 1317–1332. doi:10.1016/j.tate.2007.06.002

Schleppegrell, M. J. (2004). *The language of schooling: A functional linguistics perspective*. Mahwah, NJ: Lawrence Erlbaum.

Short, K. G., Harste, J. C., & Burke, C. (Eds.). (1996). *Creating classrooms for authors and inquirers*. Portsmouth, NH: Heinemann.

Skinner, B. F. (1976). *About behaviourism*. New York, NY: Random House.

Smith, T. M., & Ingersoll, R. M. (2004). What are the effects of induction and mentoring on beginning teacher turnover? *American Educational Research Journal, 41*(3), 681–714. doi:10.3102/00028312041003681

Slater, J. (2012). Self-advocacy and socially just pedagogy. *Disability Studies Quarterly, 32*(1). Retrieved from www.dsq-sds.org

Sleeter, C. (2008). Equity, democracy, and neoliberal assaults on teacher education. *Teaching and Teacher Education, 54*(8), 1947–1957.

Sleeter, C. E. (2009). Teacher education, neoliberalism, and social justice. In W. Ayers, T. Quinn, & D. Stovall (Eds.), *Handbook of social justice in education* (pp. 611–625). New York, NY: Routledge.

Sloan, K. (2006). Teacher identity and agency in school worlds: Beyond the all-good/all-bad discourse on accountability-explicit curriculum policies. *Curriculum Inquiry, 36*(2), 119–152. doi:10.1111/j.1467-873X.2006.00350.x

Smagorinsky, P., Gibson, N., Bickmore, S. T., Moore, C. P., & Cook, L. S. (2004). Praxis shock: Making the transition from a student-centered university program to the corporate climate of schools. *English Education, 36*(3), 214–245. Retrieved from http://www.jstor.org/stable/40173094

Solomon, R., Singer, J., Campbell, A., & Allan, A. (2011). *Brave new teachers: Doing social justice work in neo-liberal times*. Toronto, Ontario: Canadian Scholars' Press.

Stake, R. (1995). *The art of case study research*. Thousand Oaks, CA: Sage.

Stanulis, Fallona, & Pearson (2002). 'Am I doing what I am supposed to be Doing?': Mentoring novice teachers through the uncertainties and challenges of their first year of teaching. *Mentoring & Tutoring, 10*(1), 71–81. doi:10.1080/13611260220133162

Starkey, L. (2010). Supporting the digitally able beginning teacher. *Teaching and Teacher Education, 26*(7), 1429–1438. doi:10.1016/j.tate.2010.05.002

St. Pierre, E. (2000). Poststructural feminism in education: An overview. *Qualitative Studies in Education, 13*(5), 477–515. doi:10.1080/09518390050156422

St. Pierre, E. A. (2011). Post qualitatitive research: The critique and the coming after. In N. K. Denzin & Y. S. Lincoln (Eds.), *The Sage handbook of qualitative research* (4th ed., pp. 611–625). Thousand Oaks, CA: Sage.

St. Pierre, E. A., & Roulston, K. (2006). The state of qualitative inquiry: A contested science. *International Journal of Qualitative Studies in Education, 19*(6), 673–684. doi:10.1080/09518390600975644

Strom, K. (2015). Teaching as assemblage: Negotiating practice in the first year of teaching. *Journal of Teacher Education, 66*(4), 321–333. doi:10.1177/0022487115589990

Strom, K. J., & Martin, A. D. (2013). Putting philosophy to work in the classroom: Using rhizomatics to deterritorialize neoliberal thought and practice. *Studying Teacher Education, 9*(3), 219–235. doi:10.1080/17425964.2013.830970

Strom, K., Abi-Hanna, R., Dacey, C., & Duplaise, J. (2014). Exploring and connecting lines of flight. In M. Taylor & L. Coia (Eds.), *Gender, feminism, and queer theory in the self-study of teacher education practices* (pp. 31–44). Rotterdam, The Netherlands: Sense Publishing.

Taguchi, H. L. (2007). Deconstructing and transgressing the theory—Practice dichotomy in early childhood education. *Educational Philosophy and Theory, 39*(3), 275–290. doi:10.1111/j.1469-5812.2007.00324.x

Tait, M. (2008). Resilience as a contributor to novice teacher success, commitment, and retention. *Teacher Education Quarterly, 35*(4), 57–75. Retrieved from http://www.jstor.org/stable/23479174

Taylor, M., & Otinsky, G. (2007). Becoming whole language teachers and social justice agents: Pre-service teachers inquire with sixth graders. *International Journal of Progressive Education, 3*(2) 59–71.

Taylor, M., Klein, E. J., Onore, C., Strom, K., & Abrams, L. (2016). Exploring inquiry in the third space: Case studies of the first year in an urban teacher residency program. *The New Educator, 12*(3), 243–268. doi:10.1080/1547688X.2016.1187980

Thorne, J. L. S., & Lantolf, J. P. (2006). *Sociocultural theory and the genesis of second language development*. Oxford, UK: Oxford University Press.

Towers, J. (2009). Learning to teach mathematics through inquiry: A focus on the relationship between describing and enacting inquiry-oriented teaching. *Journal of Mathematics Education, 13*(3), 243–263. doi:10.1007/s10857-009-9137-9

Tuck, E., & Gorlewski, J. (2016). Racist ordering, settler colonialism, and edTPA: A participatory policy analysis. *Educational Policy, 30*(1), 197–217. doi:10.1177/0895904815616483

Tyack, D., & Tobin, W. (1994). The "grammar" of schooling: Why has it been so hard to change? *American Educational Research Journal, 31*(3), 453–479. doi:10.3102/00028312031003453

Ulvik, M., Smith, K., & Helleve, I. (2009). Novice in secondary school-the coin has two sides. *Teaching and Teacher Education, 25*(6), 835–842. doi:10.1016/j.tate.2009.01.003

U.S. Department of Education. (2002). *No child left behind*. Retrieved from http://www2.ed.gov/policy/elsec/leg/esea02/index.html

U.S. Department of Education. (2010). *Race to the top*. Retrieved from http://www2.ed.gov/programs/racetothetop-assessment/index.html

U.S. Department of Education. (2011). *Our future, our teachers: The Obama administration's plan for teacher education reform and improvement*. Retrieved from https://www.ed.gov/sites/default/files/our-future-our-teachers.pdf

Valencia, S., Martin, S., Place, N., & Grossman, P. (2009). Complex interactions in student teaching: Lost opportunities for learning. *Journal of Teacher Education, 60*(3), 304–322. doi:10.1177/0022487109336543

Veenman, S. (1984). Perceived problems of beginning teachers. *Review of Educational Research, 54*(2), 143–178. doi:10.3102/00346543054002143

Villegas, A. M. (1988). School failure and cultural mismatch: Another view. *The Urban Review, 20*(4), 253–265. doi:10.1007/BF01120137

Villegas, A. M. (1991). *Culturally responsive pedagogy for the 1990s and beyond* (Trends and Issues Paper no. 6). Washington, DC: ERIC.

Villegas, A. M. (2007). Dispositions in teacher education: A look at social justice. *Journal of Teacher Education, 58*(5), 370–380. doi: 10.1177/0022487107308419

Villegas, A. M., & Lucas, T. (2002). *Culturally responsive teaching: A coherent approach.* Albany, NY: SUNY Press.

Villegas, A. M., & Lucas, T. (2007). The culturally responsive teacher. *Educational Leadership, 64*(6), 28–33.

Villegas, A. M., & Lucas, T. (2011). A framework for linguistically responsive teaching. In T. Lucas (Ed.), *Teacher preparation for linguistically diverse classrooms: A resource for teacher educators* (pp. 55–72). New York, NY: Routledge.

Vygotsky, L. S. (1978). *Mind in society: The development of higher psychological processes.* Cambridge, MA: Harvard University Press.

Weiner, L. (2003). Why is classroom management so vexing to urban teachers? *Theory into Practice, 42*(4), 305–312. doi:10.1207/s15430421tip4204_7

Weinstein, C. S., Tomlinson-Clarke, S., & Curran, M. (2004). Toward a conception of culturally responsive classroom management. *Journal of Teacher Education, 55*(1), 25–38. doi:10.1177/0022487103259812

Wiggins, G., & McTighe, J. (2005). *Understanding by design.* Alexandria, VA: Association for Supervision and Curriculum Development.

Windschitl, M. (2002). Framing constructivism in practice as the negotiation of dilemmas: An analysis of the conceptual, pedagogical, cultural, and political challenges facing teachers. *Review of Educational Research, 72*(2), 131–175. doi:10.3102/00346543072002131

Zeichner, K. (2003). The adequacies and inadequacies of three strategies to recruit, prepare, and retain the best teachers. *Teachers College Record, 105*(3), 490–519.

Zeichner, K. (2010a). Rethinking the connections between campus courses and field experiences in college- and university-based teacher education. *Journal of Teacher Education, 61*(2), 89–99. doi:10.1177/0022487109347671

Zeichner, K. (2010b). Competition, economic rationalization, increased surveillance, and attacks on diversity: Neo-liberalism and the transformation of teacher education in the U.S. *Teaching and Teacher Education, 26*(4), 1544–1552. doi:10.1016/j.tate.2010.06.004

Zeichner, K. (2011). Assessing state and federal policies to evaluate the quality of teacher preparation programs. In P. Earley, D. Imig, & N. Michelli (Eds.), *Teacher education policy in the United States: Issues and tensions in an era of evolving expectations* (pp. 76–105). New York, NY: Routledge.

Zeichner, K. (2016). Advancing social justice and democracy in teacher education: Teacher preparation 1.0, 2.0, and 3.0. *Kappa Delta Pi Record, 52*(4), 150–155. doi:10.1080/00228958.2016.1223986

Zeichner, K., & Gore, J. (1990).Teacher socialization. In W. R. Houston (Ed.), *Handbook of research on teacher education* (pp. 329–348). New York, NY: MacMillan.

Zeichner, K., & Tabachnick, B. (1981). Are the effects of university teacher education "washed out" by school experience? *Journal of Teacher Education, 32*(3), 7–11. doi:10.1177/002248718103200302

Zembylas, M. (2003). Interrogating "teacher identity": Emotion, resistance, and self-formation. *Educational Theory, 53*(1), 107–127. doi:10.1111/j.1741-5446.2003.00107.x

Zembylas, M. (2007). The specters of bodies and affects in the classroom: A rhizo-ethological approach. *Pedagogy, Culture & Society, 15*(1), 19–35. doi:10.1080/14681360601162030